60 Days to Becoming A Smarter Manager

How to Meet Your Goals, Manage an Awesome Work Team, Create Valued Employees and Love your Job

Matilda Walsh

This workbook accompanies this book:

Table of Contents

Introduction

Congratulations, you are a team manager! Perhaps this is your first time working as a team supervisor or manager. Or perhaps you have spent time as a manager already and want to improve your management skills. Or maybe you are about to start working with a brand new team.

The goal of this book is to make you a more efficient and successful manager in 60 days.

This book will share with you the proven tips & strategies to help you become a successful manager, lead a talented team, complete all your projects successfully and impress your boss. And instead of feeling tired and burnt out, by implementing the strategies in this book you'll also feel good about turning off your laptop and leaving work on time every day, stress free and ready to spend time with family and friends.

I will help you discover and implement proven tools, tips, and strategies to become a successful manager. We will do this in two practical ways:

You will find easy strategies to implement that will help you develop a team that works great together and gets work and projects done and goals accomplished using clear processes in an efficient and organized way—so all your projects and work gets done successfully - without the drama! PLUS as a manager, you will empower people to reach their career goals while they feel valued and happy and want to stay in the company.

And as a result of creating a happy, motivated, and high-performing team that reaches all its goals, you will get to enjoy a successful management career and job satisfaction, and you will be able to leave work on time to enjoy time with your children and family.

Each week you will get five tasks to complete. In total, you will get 60 tasks over 12 weeks. If you fall behind, don't worry. Just restart that week when you are ready. Remember, the goal is to ensure that you are an effective manager with a high-performing team and balanced life.

By reading this book, you are already on your way!

What Makes a Manager Effective?

Many authors have voiced their opinions on what differentiates an effective manager from a mediocre manager. Some authors have claimed that the answer lies in certain skills or personality traits. The truth is that you can be an effective manager, provided you know yourself, your team, and the challenges you will face.

Unfortunately, the opposite is also true. If you do not consciously try to be a good manager, you may quickly fall into bad habits. In an informal poll taken among colleagues, 88% of them said that they are relieved when the manager is not in the office. Let's make sure your employees are not part of the 88%!

All effective managers do the following:

- They have honest relationships with their employees.
- Their communication is effective and non-threatening.
- Team building is a priority for them.

- They understand the financial aspects of the business.
- They create a positive work environment.
- They empower their employees.

Effective managers not only strive for greatness, but want to take their employees with them on the journey. They are not scared of being challenged or criticized and are not threatened by a strong team. In fact, they want to develop each member of the team to become an effective manager themselves in time.

If you help people get what they want, they will help you get what you want. –Zig Ziglar

A Quick Overview of Management Styles

A management style dictates how the manager will lead their team, how they will make decisions and plans, and their approach to conflict. Management styles are greatly influenced by personality—an introverted manager will have a different management style from an extroverted manager. Yet, all good managers are able to adapt their management style in response to the environment in order to achieve their goals.

There are three basic management styles:

1. Autocratic Management Styles

Autocratic leaders like to be in control, they are often micromanagers, and employees are treated as subjects that need to be instructed and monitored. These leaders are often very persuasive and it may seem that employees have been allowed to voice their opinions when in reality the decision has been made before consulting anyone.

Autocratic leaders often lead by threats and their employees live in constant fear of being taken to task. In the short term, it may seem that this kind of management style gets results, but this is not sustainable over long periods of time.

Although this management style is hostile and should be avoided, there are times of crisis where decisions need to be taken quickly and decisively and a manager may be required to step in and act in an autocratic manner for a short period. Managers should avoid being autocratic constantly as employees will find it hostile and condescending. If employees feel that they are not being heard, communication will be hampered, creativity and innovation will soon die, and productivity will start to decline.

2. Democratic Management Styles

Democratic managers encourage employees to voice their opinions, but the final decision still lies with the manager. As employees feel valued and empowered, the relationship between a manager and their employees is a positive one where mutual trust exists.

As discussions are encouraged, the employees feel free not only to express their views, but they often offer creative solutions that otherwise may have been overlooked.

Although this management style seems to work both for managers and employees, there are some drawbacks.

The biggest flaw is that it is time-consuming to get everyone's opinion every time a decision has to be made. Another is that if the manager never takes responsibility for making decisions on their own, the team may lose trust in them as a leader which will eventually lead to a breakdown of the relationship.

3. Laissez-Faire Management Styles

This is a hands-off style of management. Staff is left to make their own decisions and solve their own problems—in effect, they are their "own boss."

The manager may still assign tasks, but once the task is assigned, it is up to the employee to find the best way to complete the task and solve any challenges along the way. Once the task is completed, the manager may review the outcome and advise on amendments for future projects.

This management style is the least confrontational and may seem beneficial for both manager and employee. Unfortunately, employees may feel that the absence of leadership means the manager is negligent or inattentive.

Employees may also not feel comfortable asking the manager for assistance as they may be seen as incompetent. Thus, the team may seem cohesive (as they are struggling together), but the manager will not be seen as the leader or as part of the team, and they will remain an outsider.

There is a place and time for all three management styles, but the democratic management style should be preferred for long-term projects.

The Impact of a Bad Manager

The impact of a bad manager is far-reaching and the consequences for a company are many. It may be that employees are absent as much as they can get away with as the atmosphere at work is stressful. Eventually the employees will resign which will lead to a high staff turnover. This is one of the key indicators of bad management. Employees will also not be motivated to bring their best game and will become unproductive. The problem cuts much deeper and there are hidden costs to both individuals and businesses due to bad management.

Some of the effects on employees are:

- Mental health problems, which leads to employees not performing and taking time off work
- Negative impact on physical health
- A decline in workplace performance, as unhappy employees are unproductive employees
- A decrease in creativity and innovation
- Dwindling motivation

Uninspired employees will not be looking after clients as they should be and soon the business will feel the effect on its bottom line.

In this book, we will break down the journey to being an effective manager into 60 days (or 12 weeks). Each week will have daily discussions, tips, and exercises to assist you in developing your own blueprint to being the best manager you can be.

Week 1: The Importance of Good Relationships

Taking into account that we often spend most of our waking hours with our work colleagues, it is clear that having good relationships is essential for employee well-being. If an employee is happy and relaxed at work, they will be productive and engaged. The more cohesive a team is, the higher performance rises. But as with all good things in life—building and maintaining relationships is hard work!

Any relationship is built on trust, and the relationship between a manager and the team working with them is no different. The team needs to trust the manager not only to lead them, but to take ultimate responsibility for the team's performance—to "have their backs."

Another important building block in any relationship is respect—respect for the person, the work that they do, and the unique gifts that they bring to the team.

People who feel respected will also feel safe and will trust the manager to act in their best interest. In a team environment, the leader (or manager) should lead by example. Treating team members with respect means:

- listening to their opinions
- empathizing with their perspective, even if you do not agree
- in a conflict situation, addressing the issue and not the person
- apologizing when you are wrong
- showing appreciation for their efforts
- complimenting achievements without feeling threatened

Relationships are built on open communication. Where employees do not have the confidence to voice their opinions and needs, the relationship quickly becomes very one-sided and the employee will disengage.

Daily Tips for Building Good Work Relationships

Day 1: Get to Know Each Other

Do you know your employees' personal circumstances? Do you know if they are married, have children, where they live and what their hobbies are? If you do not know, how will you be able to connect and motivate the employee? It is a good idea to have a one-on-one meeting with every team member once a week. In the meeting, the employees need to feel that they can openly discuss any challenges they experience (be it at work or home). As a manager you need to take notice of anything that may influence work performance.

Although you want employees to feel that you are "part of the team," it is not a good idea to focus too much on socializing with them. Instead—show a real interest in them as people, and make sure you connect on a deeper level so that your team members feel valued and heard. If you become "one of them" you will lose authority and your leadership position.

Remember, happy and satisfied employees are productive and will contribute to the stability and success of your business.

Today's Exercise:

Let's talk: Pick a team member you normally do not spend much time talking to. This may be a person you typically don't deal directly with. Have a short chat, and ask how they are. Are they enjoying the work? Any issues? Let them know you appreciate their work.

Day 2: Feedback Is Important

Your focus as a manager should be on the development of each person, focusing on their career path. Again, if you don't know your employees, you will not know what their ambitions and career goals are. If a job is well done, give the praise it deserves. Build your team's morale by appreciating their efforts and motivating them to reach for even greater heights.

When criticism is needed, be honest and address the issue. Your criticism should be aimed at resolving an issue and never be a personal attack. Reassure the employee that you will assist them in correcting their mistakes and that you believe they can do better in the future. The employee needs to feel that you are approachable and if they experience a problem in the future that they can knock on your door for assistance.

Today's Exercise:

Encourage a team member: Pick one team member who has been struggling. Have a private, but informal conversation with them about how they are—keep it general. How are they finding work?

Is there anything you can do to help them? Show kindness, show empathy, and try to understand their perspective. Keep it light and positive, as the goal is to gain more information on their situation so you can understand them better.

Day 3: Body Language Is Important

When meeting someone for the first time, you have 30 seconds to make an impression, so make those precious seconds count!

Words only convey 7% of our message, and tone of voice contributes 38%, but body language makes up 55% of what people perceive (Mehrabian, 1981). During the COVID-19 pandemic, many people were forced to work from home and attend meetings virtually. Without the opportunity to read someone's body language or facial expressions (mask-wearing was compulsory), communication was often strained and misunderstandings were common. We were made aware once again of how important nonverbal clues are in communicating with each other.

Think of the potential employee in an interview, shaking slightly, voice unsteady and arms and legs crossed. As an interviewer, one will pick up on the queues and the person will be perceived as incapable and anxious. Compare them to someone walking into the interview room with a smile, firm handshake, and positive body language which signals trust and proficiency. Which one will you hire?

The use of body language is often unconscious—you fold your arms or cross your legs in response to a threatening environment without thinking. But if you can consciously adopt a body language that is positive and inviting, you will find that listeners are more open to what you say and your words will have a greater impact.

Today many of our meetings are carried out virtually and we need to adapt our body language. It is important to remember that part of what you are communicating in a virtual meeting is your environment. If you can hear children screaming or a cat appears suddenly on your lap, it may seem unprofessional (unless you know the attendees very well). What you wear and how you look is always sending a message and it is not good enough to make excuses for an unprofessional appearance—you need to step it up.

Today's Exercise:

Free candy: Put a large box of candy or toffees on your desk. Invite anyone who stops by to take a candy. Word will travel fast. This is a great way to have more organic conversations with your team. The goal is to let you seem approachable and easy to talk to.

Day 4: Teamwork Is Critcal

Encourage your team members to cooperate with each other, as a team that understands and respects each other will excel. Never encourage competition between team members, but rather use the good performance of one team member to inspire the rest of the team. That is not to say that hard work should not be acknowledged and rewarded individually—but not by playing members of a team against each other.

Appreciation is an effective way to build any relationship. If a person feels valued in a relationship, they are more likely to invest energy to maintain the relationship. In a work environment, strong relationships in a team lead to greater productivity. Where team members have different roles and job descriptions, it is vital that every member of the team feels that the role they play contributes to the team's success. As a manager, you need to make sure all team members feel that they are equally important for the team to succeed.

When a team is experiencing challenges, it is important that you as the manager avoid placing blame or putting additional pressure on the team in order to improve performance as this could have the opposite effect. Ask open-ended questions in order to encourage discussion—you need to understand exactly what they are experiencing before trying to resolve the issue. You as the manager should understand the challenges your team faces, even if you don't agree with their perception of the challenge. The team may feel that they cannot perform due to operational issues, but you as manager may know that the company is facing financial constraints and that the team needs to make do with what they have. You will need to sit down with the team, explain the challenge that you are facing, and find a solution or at least come to a compromise on how to proceed.

If you have to criticize, focus on the issue and communicate in such a way that the other person does not feel threatened and needs to defend themself. Remember you are trying to resolve an issue and not proving a point. Encouragement and working together toward a solution will have a much better outcome than putting pressure and blame on team members. Remember, we are all creatures driven by emotion—criticism can wound deeply and damage relationships permanently.

Today's Exercise:

Say thank you: Say thank you at least once a day to someone for the next five days. Many people at work can feel undervalued or not appreciated. A simple thank you is a great way to address this.

Day 5: Do Not Label Employees

It is very easy to fall into the trap of labeling employees. If an individual is known (and labeled) to always complain, other team members will avoid the person, which will have a negative effect on the team. If you give someone a negative label (even if it is only in your head), you will interact with the person according to the label. For example, in your interaction with someone you have labeled as a complainer, you will expect criticism and push-back which in turn may cause you to come over unnecessarily harsh.

Another habit that will be detrimental to any team is office gossip and politics. As a manager you should never be pulled into discussing other employees or team members with anyone. Office gossip can quickly turn ugly and ruin relationships and even careers. If you have an issue with a team member, address it personally without anyone else being involved. If there is a conflict situation between two members of the team and one member complains to you, do not take sides. Listen, but do not react, and then get both members of the team to put their grievances on the table with the other person present in a non-confronting manner. Remember, you are seeking a solution to their challenge, you are not taking sides. By staying objective and really listening, you should be able to resolve the issue to the satisfaction of both employees.

Today's Exercise:

Welcome to the team: Pick the newest team member. Have a short chat. Ask how they are. Are they enjoying the work? Any issues? Let them know you appreciate their work.

A Few Last Words on Communication

As a manager, you need to be able to step back and look objectively at your own behavior and communication style and adapt it as necessary for the team to thrive. In other words, you need high emotional intelligence. Below are a few things to focus on in order to increase your emotional intelligence:

- Understanding yourself: Your own strengths and weaknesses, your needs and wants, and your goals and expectations.
- Regulate your emotions: Be aware of how you are feeling and how your emotions influence your actions. Be present in the moment, and do not let your bad mood bleed into your work environment.
- Understanding others: What makes them tick? What do they need from you to flourish? What should you avoid when interacting with them? Their dreams, needs, and goals are important.
- Social skills: The way in which you communicate, how you handle conflict, and how you solve problems are all skills that can be learned and improved.

Effective communication skills are vital for you as a manager, but should be nurtured in your employees as well. When people feel that they are heard and can voice their opinions, they are satisfied and productive. An effective manager will communicate in such a way that their employees feel safe and unthreatened. As well, they will understand their different personalities and act accordingly.

Strong communicators are strong managers—they can delegate tasks, manage conflict, and motivate their team to greater heights. Effective communication is a skill that needs to be learned and practiced. Make sure that you are putting in the necessary work to become a strong communicator.

Week 2: Impressing Your Manager

The key to climbing the corporate ladder faster often lies with your own superior. Your manager will influence your career path by promoting you (or not) and they will influence your finances, as the decision about bonuses and salary increases often lie with them. Therefore it is important to be in their good books, but you don't want to alienate your coworkers or team members by looking as if you are groveling. You need to find a balance and ways to impress your boss without looking desperate. Below you will find a tip and exercise for each day.

Daily Tips for Impressing Your Manager

Day 1: Get to Know Your Manager

We tend to forget that our managers are also human. They have dreams, aspirations, and a life away from the office.

By showing real interest in their welfare and circumstances, you will become more than just a member of the team. Most managers also report to a structure (be it a boss, owner, or shareholder) to which they are accountable. They are often buffering their teams from the pressure they experience and this can take its toll. By making your manager aware that you see them as a person and not part of the process flow, you will go a long way in being remembered when they need to make decisions about your career path.

By initiating conversations about your manager's vision for their department (or company) you can get a better understanding of your own role and growth opportunities. If you can align your expectations with that of your manager it will avoid conflict and disillusionment in the future. You may envision yourself as a senior manager in two years, but by talking to your superior, you may discover this will only be on the cards in five years. You can plan better if you know what to expect in the short and long terms.

Today's Exercise:

Evaluate expectations: Schedule a meeting with your manager to evaluate their expectations.

Ask them what the goals are that they want you to achieve in your job in the next month, the next six months, and the next year.

Day 2: Feedback Preferences

The term “feedback” refers to all information supplied in connection with a process to the individual responsible. Feedback can be instantaneous, as in a dissatisfied customer complaining about their shopping experience, or it can be information gathered over time, for example, a performance evaluation with an individual.

Every person has a preferred way to communicate with their team (and therefore to receive feedback). Some managers prefer to put everything in writing to minimize misunderstandings while others prefer a quick one-on-one chat or a phone call. Your manager will also want feedback from you and you need to determine how often this should occur and what format they prefer. Even though it may seem intimidating, it is better to stay in touch with your manager constantly.

In this way, you will be sure to be made aware should there be any challenges or expectations that are not managed. For example, if you have a sales target of 100 items over a three-month period.

You will feel more comfortable if you have feedback from your manager regularly to say if you are on track or if you need to pick up your performance. If you experience challenges, it is also easier to address them with a manager who has been part of the process than with someone who only gets involved periodically.

If your boss prefers to discuss decisions face-to-face, but then forgets what you discussed, it may be helpful to send an email after the meeting outlining the points of discussion and the conclusion. Reminding them in writing will not only prompt them to act, but will eliminate future misunderstandings based on "that is not what I said or meant." Many conflict situations at the office can be avoided by clear communication.

It is also important to find out what our feedback should look like. You may be preparing a presentation with graphs and conclusions while your boss is actually looking for a simple spreadsheet.

Today's Exercise:

Feedback facts: Ask your manager what format they prefer and how often they require feedback. Is it daily?

Or Tuesdays and Fridays? Do they want to meet with you in person, or on the phone, or is an email sufficient? When will you have catch-up meetings—weekly or monthly?

Day 3: Schedule Reminders

No manager likes to remind employees about tasks that need to be completed or feedback that is late. A very quick way to lose your manager's trust is by ignoring deadlines or being late constantly. Being on time for work and submitting assignments on time shows that you can be trusted and are capable of doing your job. If you have multiple projects running at the same time, prioritize and make sure that every project is completed before its deadline.

This is also applicable to being on time for work. An employee who is constantly late for work is sending out the message that they do not respect their manager's and colleagues' time and that they would rather be elsewhere. If you know that the traffic is more congested on certain days of the week, make sure to set your alarm clock to go off earlier. All managers will have sympathy for an employee who is late once in a while, but if it is a constant occurrence, you may well face disciplinary action.

Stay ahead of your to-do list by scheduling reminders before the time. If you need to send in a weekly report on Fridays, schedule a recurring reminder for Thursday morning to give you enough time to prepare for the task.

There is no excuse for missing deadlines or being late with all the reminders that are available on your calendar, on your phone, and if you are lucky, Siri or Alexa can remind you verbally.

Today's Exercise:

Remember not to forget: Schedule a to-do list item in your calendar to set up these reminders for your manager, so that the manager does not need to remind you.

Day 4: Go the Extra Mile

If you really want to stand out in the colleague "crowd," be prepared to take on more than what is expected of you. If you see a task that needs to be completed and no one is taking responsibility, step up and volunteer to do it. It may have nothing to do with your job description—the tea lady may be away sick and the dishes are stacking up—be the one to wash up. You may know that a colleague is falling behind on a project, so volunteer to assist—in other words, be the one "who picks up the slack." You may think that your manager is unaware of this, but a manager with their ear to the ground will soon know who the people are that they can rely on to "go the extra mile."

Going the extra mile is not only applicable to taking responsibility for additional tasks, but constantly delivering more than what is asked of you. There may be times when the team is under pressure and your manager requires you to put in overtime or work from home. Accept the responsibility with a positive attitude—if you can be counted on in times of crisis, your manager will remember it when the time for reward comes.

But going the extra mile comes with a caveat. If you are constantly picking up the slack for other people or volunteering for a job no one else wants to do, you will soon become the doormat of the office. You will be expected to wash the dishes or complete someone else's project. Thus, it is important to establish boundaries. After you have done the dishes say something like, “Today I had my turn. Who is standing in tomorrow?” After assisting the colleague with their project tell him, “I am sure next time you will know what to do and when to start to make the deadline.”

Today’s Exercise:

Managers’ little helper: Ask your manager what else you could do to help them. Make a note of their answer and implement it.

Day 5: Be a Problem Solver

Most of us are quick to complain and we can identify challenges and reasons why something will not work. This is not what your manager needs. They need a team member who cannot only identify the problem, but who also can come up with solutions. A positive "can-do" attitude will go a long way in making you an indispensable team member.

To solve problems, there are a few basic steps to follow:

- Determine the exact cause of the problem.
    - What causes the issue? The real cause of the problem may sometimes not be clear. For example, your team not making their sales target may seem like a performance issue, but on investigation, you may find that the cause is that they do not have the necessary equipment to do their job effectively, which means the problem is actually operational.
- Find solutions to the problem.
    - Here you need to put on your innovative thinking cap and think of a different approach to find a solution to the problem. The solution needs to be

practical, scalable, and with as little risk as possible. Results will also have to be measurable against the previous process to make sure that the solution is really a step in the right direction.

- Once you have decided on a workable solution, you need to plan the processes needed to implement the plan. This will be the blueprint you will present to your manager.

Today's Exercise:

Fix it: The next time you approach your manager with an issue, also bring two possible solutions to fix it.

Week 3: Make Meetings Short and Fun

In an era where there are so many ways of communicating we may ask if meetings are still necessary—and the answer is YES! While emails and communication platforms (like Slack, WhatsApp, and others) are crucial, we may risk losing "the human touch" in entirely eliminating meetings (be they face-to-face or virtual).

Meetings are commonly used to share important information with employees and to get real-time feedback. A meeting is a great place to share good news and to celebrate achievements. After the celebrations may be the right time to set new goals or targets as employees are in a positive mindset.

A meeting is also an ideal setting for feedback and updates from different departments or employees. This may lead to organic discussions and even a brainstorming session where valuable new processes and ideas are born.

Where challenges are discussed, meetings may quickly get heated. It is your responsibility as a manager to maintain order and keep the discussion on point.

Daily Tips to Have Effective Meetings

Day 1: What Works and What Doesn't?

Every company and department is unique. What works for one should not be enforced without thought upon another. Situations also change and as a manager, you should be able to adapt to the current needs of your employees. Below are a couple of meeting types commonly used. Your company may have its own needs and processes and may use these in combination.

- Decision-making meetings: These are often called on short notice and require input from the attendees regarding the road forward. These may be operational issues that may be urgent to resolve or where the group needs to take action in order to perform.

- Problem-solving meetings: These are held when a specific issue impacts employees and a decision needs to be made for a solution. Feedback is required from all involved in order to resolve the issue to everyone's satisfaction.
- Team-building meetings: Most employees enjoy this type of meeting most as it involves a fun team-building activity. The meeting need not take place in a formal setting, but can be held outside or in a coffee shop. No formal agenda (except for the activity planned) and loads of time for socializing are key points for a successful team-building event. As a manager, you will need to keep an eye on employees not included spontaneously in the activities and take extra care to make them feel part of the team.
- Brainstorming meetings: These are best scheduled well in advance and with proper warning as you want your team to come prepared and with innovative ideas. The purpose of this meeting is for the team to share and discuss their ideas as a starting point. Usually, the meeting quickly evolves away from the original ideas brought to the table and new and creative concepts are born.
- One-on-one meetings: This type of meeting is to be scheduled between two people to discuss a specific topic. This is not the informal office chat taking place at

the watercooler, but a formal meeting where preparation may be necessary. Typically, performance meetings with employees will take this form. Remember, it is your task as a manager to make the person you are meeting comfortable. Do not jump right into the discussion, but ask about the employee's welfare and make small talk at the start of the meeting. This type of meeting may be intimidating and daunting to employees if not handled correctly.

- Planning meetings: These may be held weekly, monthly, quarterly, and yearly and are aimed at planning and setting the necessary processes in place in order to achieve the required goals. There may be limited feedback and discussion, but the chairman should have a clear idea of the information they want to convey.
- Check-in meetings: This is usually a regularly scheduled meeting (for example, every day just before going home). It is a short meeting to recap the day and plan for tomorrow. If any issues are raised, a problem-solving meeting may need to be scheduled.

Today's Exercise:

Meeting types: Identify what meetings you attend work well and which ones do not. Analyze what works and what does not work.

Day 2: Get the Meeting Moving

The trend of walking meetings or “walk and talk” meetings has taken the world by storm. We all know that walking gets the blood pumping, but did you know that it also gets the creative juices flowing? Feedback suggests that walking meetings lead to more honest exchanges with employees. This makes sense as the walking partners are literally “on equal footing” without someone sitting at the top of the boardroom table.

A study by The Harvard Business Review (Clayton et al., 2015) looked at 150 working adults in the U.S. They found that 5.25% of the study group reported feeling more creative in their jobs if they participated in walking meetings. A further 8.5% reported that they feel more focused and engaged in their jobs. These may not seem to be numbers that will have a huge impact on a business, but over time they will make a difference. Furthermore, it is beneficial for employees' health to get walking and step out of the office, and all of this is at no cost to the business.

Tips on how to have a successful walking meeting:

- Take a pen and notebook with you, and write down any ideas or concerns you may need to address in a formal meeting.
- Inform colleagues or clients in advance if you plan a walking meeting so that everyone involved can dress comfortably. Be sensitive that not everyone may be comfortable (or able) to attend a walking meeting.
- Walking meetings are intended for meeting one-on-one, so the group should not exceed three people, as if it does, the group would automatically split into smaller units and discussion would become impossible.
- Walking meetings should not replace formal meetings and participation should remain voluntary at all times.

Today's Exercise:

Walk and talk: Schedule a meeting with a colleague to get some exercise and fresh air. Remember to keep the tips given above in mind.

Day 3: Stand and Meet

Another "meeting innovation" is standing meetings. Many big companies (such as Google and Forbes) have realized that the conventional way of conducting a meeting may not be the most productive. The main advantage of meeting standing up is the attendees remain more alert and focused and the meeting tends to be shorter and more to the point. This type of meeting discourages unnecessary discussion and encourages participation. Neal Taparia, Co-CEO of Easy Solutions, shares that his employees are more mindful and less preoccupied in standing meetings. Standing meetings should be limited to 30 minutes.

Standing meetings may be informal, as in quickly planning the day first thing in the morning. But shorter, more formal meetings will also work well. No special office equipment is necessary, but it may be beneficial to have a standing table to make it possible for attendees to make notes during the meeting. A big flip board or smart technology may be used effectively during standing meetings.

Advantages of standing meetings:

- Attendees are more alert and focused.
- Shorter meeting times make standing meetings more efficient.
- Distractions (such as emails and phone calls) are eliminated.
- Attendees feel engaged and included.
- Beneficial to the health of attendees.
- An increased sense of team cohesiveness.

Today's Exercise:

Stand up and talk: Schedule one standing meeting. See how short this meeting can be while achieving all your goals.

Day 4: Public Praise

A proverb says, “Praise in public, criticize in private.” This is a good motto to remember during meetings. Public praise is an excellent way to raise the morale of the team, spread appreciation, and motivate and encourage your team.

Praise can be doled out at any meeting, but it works best in check-in meetings where feedback is required from team members. When a team member has delivered above-expected performance, this is the time for praise and to show appreciation. It may also give an opportunity to have the achiever share their secret with the rest of the team to motivate them to the same heights.

Company-wide meetings where all teams and departments give feedback on progress or project status are natural platforms that can be used to acknowledge and celebrate outstanding performance. If the outstanding performance is awarded on the spot, it will have even a greater impact.

Another creative platform for praise is to have a meeting just before leaving for the weekend. A "cheers of peers" meeting leaves everyone feeling good when leaving the office for the weekend. This celebration should not only be reserved for work-related performance, but can be used to encourage and recognize team members for their contributions. For example, if a new member of the team has made their first sale, celebrate it. The coworker getting engaged or buying a new house also has reason to celebrate. Once in a while, ask your team to make a list of what they appreciate in each of the other team members and read the comments allowed—there is no greater motivation than to know that you are valued as a person.

Examples of how to give praise to employees:

- *"A big shout out to William for staying late on Tuesday to complete the project. Your hard work and dedication set an example for all of us."*
- *"Let's give a hand to Martha for achieving her target for the second week running. You are a star, Martha!"*

Keep the praise short, light and humorous, as extended speeches of appreciation may be embarrassing for the recipient.

Remember to not only celebrate individuals, but team performance as well. When a project is finished successfully or targets are reached, give praise and celebrate as a team. If you are able to reward the team for work well done, do so. This need not cost money, but could be as simple as going home an hour earlier on a Friday. It is not always the reward, but often the thought, that carries the most weight.

Today's Exercise:

Praise for peers: In one meeting, praise one or more team members publicly for a job well done.

Day 5: Meeting Protocols

In a time where many meetings are informal and the format may vary from traditional meetings to walking or standing meetings, it is important to take note of a formal meeting's protocol. There are meetings where protocol is still strictly adhered to and you as a manager should be able to step into these meetings with confidence. Meetings where a formal protocol is still followed include board and shareholder meetings.

- A formal meeting notice or request to attend will be sent out well in advance. You need to respond to the request promptly. The notice or request will often contain the agenda for the meeting in order to allow attendees to prepare.
- Someone (usually a secretary or personal assistant) will be responsible to take the minutes of the meeting. The minutes will include the time and date of the meeting and the names of the attendees. Points of discussion will be noted. The minutes will conclude with an action plan and persons responsible as well as when the next meeting will take place and any questions raised that need further discussion.

- Start the meeting on time. Delaying the meeting to wait for late arrivals may seem disrespectful to those who took the effort to be on time. Ask attendees to silence or switch off their cellphones to minimize distractions.
- The agenda should be in writing and handed out to every attendee at the start of the meeting. The agenda should also be included in the invitation that is sent out.
- Open the meeting by welcoming the attendees and briefly stating the purpose of the meeting. If the attendees do not know each other, introduce yourself first and then introduce them to each other (include a short description of their job title and why they are attending the meeting). For example, “On my right, we have Mr. John Smith. He is our company's Financial Manager and will advise on the feasibility of the project we are discussing today.”
- Work through the agenda point by point. Encourage discussion, as a meeting should not be a one-sided lecture, and input from all attendees is required. If you know that one of your team members is knowledgeable on the subject, but not speaking up, ask them for their opinion by name. Limit the time for discussion for each item on the agenda. The meeting should be kept as short as possible. Rather schedule follow-up meetings with the stakeholders involved.

- Conclude the meeting with a short summary of what has been discussed and what actions are needed. Thank all attendees for their time and attendance.

Some of the things that need to be avoided during formal meetings are interrupting a speaker even if you strongly disagree, and straying from the agenda. Never share information of what has been discussed with colleagues not invited to the meeting, unless specifically asked to.

Today's Exercise:

Follow protocol: Schedule one meeting and arrange the following:

1. Set an agenda and share it before the meeting.
2. Designate a note-taker.
3. Actively include remote attendees.
4. Start and end the meeting on time.
5. End the meeting with an action plan.

6.

Week 4: Motivate and Inspire

We are not a team because we work together. We are a team because we respect, trust, and care for each other. –Vala Afsar

The best managers are employee focused and understand the importance of keeping their teams motivated to achieve the best results. Result-oriented managers who use tactics like fear and threats may have short-term results, but over time they will not only damage their credibility as leaders, but productivity will decline and staff turnover will increase. A manager's goal should be to have a sustainable performance from a gratified team.

In times of change, a confident manager who inspires their team to accept the changes with a positive attitude will find fewer disruptions in performance from their team. Your team is looking at you for guidance, motivation, and inspiration.

In the next week, we will look at a few ways you can become better at this.

Daily Tips to Motivate and Inspire Your Team

Day 1: Get in the Trenches

A manager who sits on the sideline and criticizes will be resented by their team as they will feel that they do not understand the challenges they face. They may disregard practical advice the manager offers as they may feel that they cannot offer an opinion on something they have not experienced.

The most successful managers (even in the C-suite) are those who have come through the ranks before succeeding. There is a reason successful entrepreneurs do not just appoint family members in key positions, but require them to prove themselves by climbing the corporate ladder before arriving at the corner office.

If your team has a project deadline and they need to work late or over weekends to complete the project, join them. Become part of the team and work with them. You may bring skills to the table that may make the difference between finishing on time and missing a deadline. If the team sees that you have their backs and are willing to dirty your hands, they will not only trust you, but you will build an incredibly strong, loyal, and cohesive team.

If you did not come through the ranks in your current company it may be a good idea to spend a day shadowing each member of your team to get a better idea of what their day looks like. Once you understand their day, you will better be able to adjust processes for maximum performance.

Today's Exercise:

Help out: Take one task and help out a team member. Get your hands dirty. If they have to stay late, you stay late too, to help them. Do something to prove to your team that you are all in it together.

Day 2: Charity or Volunteer Work

We all know that the people on the receiving end of the charity gain from the effort. They aren't, after all, the ones receiving funds, food, or something they desperately need, but did you know that charity workers call what they feel after helping out the "happiness effect?"

Helping others ignites our happiness. A study by the London School of Economics (2021) suggests that the more people volunteer, the happier they are. Feeling needed and feeling that you are a contributing member of society not only increases self-confidence, but combats depression. Volunteering is not a solitary activity and forces not only interaction with others, but often provides an additional support system as co-volunteers quickly become friends. Many psychologists are now recognizing the positive effect volunteering has on our mental health and are encouraging patients suffering from depression to get involved.

Apart from the mental advantages of volunteering it also helps you to stay active and healthy. Volunteer work can be a welcome escape from your day-to-day routine and may provide you with energy, creativity, and motivation that can be carried over to your personal and work lives.

Today's Exercise:

Show support: Research a charity that your company supports. Identify someone on your team who would like to arrange a morning cake sale. All proceeds are to go to charity. They will pick a date, time, and location. Put up posters and encourage people to bring in cakes. Afterward, you will announce how much was raised for the charity and thank the organizer and everyone who made and brought cakes.

Day 3: Pick Their Brains

Your employees are geniuses, so pick their brains. Great leaders understand that they are not the only people capable of making good decisions or coming up with innovative ideas. To increase office morale, tell your employees you are always open to hearing their ideas. And turn the right ones into reality.
–Son, 2016

A good manager (and leader) understands that their team may have skills and knowledge they lack. If you as a manager are responsible to appoint team members, choose team members that fill the voids you may have. Do not be scared to choose people who have stronger skillsets than you in certain areas, as you are building a strong team and you need strong members.

Do not be scared to ask for advice or input from members who have more experience or knowledge on a subject than you have. You will not be losing face, but you set an example of being open to learning something new. Remember, asking for input and listening to others does not mean you need to follow their advice or bend to their opinion. In the end, the decision still lies with you. Ask questions like, "What do you think we should do?" and not "What should we do?"

Be open to learning new skills or broadening your field of knowledge. Showing openness to learn is one of the crucial qualities when climbing the corporate ladder. If you are also aspiring to a higher position, it will only enhance your employability. By involving your team in solving a problem you not only show that you value their input, but also that you trust their knowledge and skills to address the issue.

Today's Exercise:

Show me how: Identify an operational issue you have in the office and ask your team to come up with a creative and workable solution. Discuss the pros and cons of their suggested solution and if the pros outweigh the cons, implement it.

Day 4: Let Us Celebrate

Most of us enjoy celebrating our birthdays, this is the one day of the year that you should be the center of attention. Unfortunately, most of us will also be spending the day at the office. You as a manager can use this opportunity to celebrate your team members individually—not for what they do or achieve, but simply for who they are.

There are some pivotal days in the year for most of us, and birthdays are right at the top. No wonder an employee is more likely to resign on their birthday than on any other day of the year. If that birthday is a milestone birthday (when a person turns 30, 40, or 50), the risk is even higher. This is an opportunity to show your employees that you value them, and a celebration is in order.

The benefits of celebrating an employee's birthday include increased loyalty which in turn will lead to improved work performance and an increase in job satisfaction and happiness—both factors employees consider when they resign.

There are a few tips for having successful birthday celebrations in the office:

- Keep it personal, write a personal message in a specially brought birthday card, and include a personal message to make the person feel extra special.
- Celebrate everyone's birthday in the same way. Do not pick favorites or achievers in your team for celebrations.
- Be considerate as not all people celebrate birthdays or some people do not like to celebrate publicly. Ask each team member how they would like to celebrate when they start on the job.
- If you plan on giving a gift to the employee, ask what they like or need.
- Do not share someone's age without their consent.

Whether you chose to celebrate by decorating someone's desk, having lunch, or pooling money to buy a special gift, you are celebrating someone's life with them.

Today's Exercise:

Happy birthday: Find out when everyone's birthdays are. On their birthday, surprise them with a cake and sing *Happy Birthday* as a team together.

Day 5: Organize a Fun Activity

People rarely succeed unless they have fun in what they are doing. –Dale Carnegie.

Research has shown that happy people are productive people (Sgroi, 2015). People report themselves to feel happy, are more motivated and more productive, and are less likely to be anxious or withdrawn. Happy people are more likely to engage with others and less likely to suffer from mental health issues.

Some of the advantages of a team having fun together are

- Learning to trust each other: Team members need to know that they fall back on each other in times of crisis. If you know that someone has your back, you feel safe. When a team member feels that they can trust their team, they will be more willing to open up. This will lead to greater collaboration and communication and ultimately to improved performance by the team.
- Encourages creativity: Teams taking part in fun activities together, especially if the activity requires innovative thinking (such as an escape room activity), will find that teammates can come up with creative

ideas to solve a problem. This will lead to more collaboration within the team.

- Teach acceptance: When having fun together, the traditional gender and social boundaries are broken down, and we just see each other as people. Team members may realize that their preconceived ideas about certain team members were unfounded and unfair. A team with members who appreciate each other is a strong team.

Today's Exercise:

Have some fun: Plan an exciting after-hours activity that your employees will look forward to. Ask someone on your team to ask everyone and come up with five different ideas. See if your company will sponsor one of them.

Week 5: Sleep, Hydration, and Health

Daily Tips to Take Care of Your body

Day 1: The Benefits of Sleep

To sleep is not a choice, as all living things need to sleep and it is an essential function. Many functions in your body only take place while you are asleep. Sleep is also the time your mind processes what happened during the day. Without enough sleep, your body cannot function optimally. Sleep deprivation will lead to a reduced ability to concentrate, slower reactions, and altered moods. Sleep-deprived people also have a higher risk of developing certain medical conditions such as obesity, type 2 diabetes, and high blood pressure.

Every person has an "internal body clock" that regulates when we wake up (without an alarm) and when we want to go to sleep. This clock is also known as the circadian rhythm and its cycle spans 24 hours. There are many influences on our circadian rhythm (such as hormones, sugar levels, and activity during the day), but the most important is light. As the sun sets, our bodies produce more melatonin (the sleep hormone) that makes us drowsy. Unfortunately, modern humans are bombarded with artificial light and our circadian rhythms are affected. This is the reason it is important to turn off all screens emitting light at least 30 minutes before going to sleep. According to the Sleep Foundation (2022), a healthy adult between 26 and 64 years of age needs seven to nine hours of sleep a night.

Today's Exercise:

Track your sleep: Download an application to track your sleep patterns. Track your sleep for seven days.

Day 2: New Bedtime Routine

To get the correct amount of sleep, you need to establish a bedtime routine that works for you. You should try to stick to your bedtime routine, even over weekends and holidays, for the best results. Many people find that writing the next day's to-do list before starting the bedtime routine assists in clearing the mind of worries about things that need to be done the following day.

Tips for better sleep:

- Stick to a bedtime, keeping in mind that you need at least seven hours of sleep.
- Have a light snack or bedtime tea (such as chamomile or lavender).
- Listen to relaxing music.
- Do relaxation techniques (such as stretching or breathing exercises).
- Your bedroom should be at a comfortable temperature.
- Make sure your pillow, mattress, and bedding are comfortable.
- Ban all screens from the bedroom at least 30 minutes before bedtime.

- Do not drink caffeine or alcohol in the hours leading up to bedtime.
- Try not to eat large meals two hours before going to bed.
- Exercise during the day will assist in healthy sleep, but exercise too close to bedtime will delay sleep. Do not exercise just before bedtime.
- Read a good book for 30 minutes before falling asleep.

Today's Exercise:

Change your routine: Take note of what you do before going to sleep. Try to stay off your phone and social media, and do not drink coffee just before bedtime. Read a book for 30 minutes before you sleep. Implement the new bedtime routine and track your progress by continuing with the sleep application.

Day 3: Drink Enough Water

According to an article published by Dr. Jillian Kubala in *Medical News Today* (Kubala, 2020), the human body is composed of around 60% water. All of our body functions are dependent on water. These include digestion, blood circulation, lubrication of joints, brain function, the creation of saliva to assist with speech and consuming food, maintaining a healthy temperature, and waste removal (through sweat, urine, and bowel movements). Water is so important to our well-being that we would die of dehydration if we did not take in fluids within three days.

Apart from the critical functions facilitated by water, there are many additional advantages to taking in enough water daily. Water helps with calorie intake as it combats hunger pains by making your stomach feel full. Foods with a higher water content take longer to get absorbed by the body and thus make us feel full longer.

Water is essential in maintaining a healthy electrolyte level. This is the level of salts and minerals in your blood responsible for conducting electrical impulses in the body. If the electrolyte balance is faulty, it may become dangerous and even life-threatening as the heart will not be able to function properly.

On a more cosmetic note, water is essential for our skin to look healthy. Dehydrated skin is more likely to appear flaky and wrinkled. Below are some tips to help you drink more fluids:

- Have a glass of water with every meal.
- Eat more fruits and vegetables as they are high in water.
- Keep a bottle of water in your car, at your desk, and next to your bed.

Today's Exercise:

How many glasses?: Keep track of your daily fluid intake. Buy a large water bottle and fill it with water. Your goal is to drink one full bottle a day.

Day 4: Use Water to Relax

Many people know instinctively that water has a calming effect on their anxious minds. Now, science has proven this as a fact (Russel, 2013). We go on holiday to lay on the beach to watch the waves break or sit next to a lagoon to watch the water. Psychologists call this the "blue health" phenomenon.

One would think that since humans can easily drown, submerging in water should be experienced as a threat. The opposite is true, as when a person's face is submerged, their heart rate slows down and the body's "fight-or-flight" responses are quietened. This is known as the "dive reflex" and is well documented. This reflex is so predictable that it has been used by emergency doctors to treat certain heart arrhythmias and extreme panic attacks. Use this to your advantage by taking a long bath in times of anxiety.

Today's Exercise:

Take note of any large bodies of water near you.

It may be the sea, a lake, or a dam. You may even pass over a river on your way to work. Make time to pause and appreciate it, and note how it makes you feel. When taking a bath or shower, be aware of how the water on your skin makes you feel.

Day 5: Schedule a Health Check With Your Doctor

When last did you have a check-up with the doctor? Our bodies, like car engines, need regular check-ups and maintenance.

During a regular check-up, the doctor starts by measuring your height and weight. This will be used to determine your body mass index (BMI). Your BMI should fall within a healthy range, as a BMI that is too high may indicate a higher risk profile for heart disease and diabetes type 2 as well as some cancers, while a too low BMI may place you at risk of suffering from diseases such as osteoporosis and a compromised immune function.

Your doctor will also measure your blood pressure. Normal blood pressure is 120 over 80 or below. High blood pressure is 130 over 80 or higher. High blood pressure put you at risk of heart disease and possible stroke and should be monitored closely.

Cholesterol is a type of fat in the blood and may lead to heart attack and stroke. Your doctor will most likely do a finger prick test in their office to determine your cholesterol. If they are concerned about the result or if you are an older overweight male patient, they may send you for more detailed blood tests to look at the different cholesterol counts.

Blood sugar can also be measured in the doctor's office by using a finger prick test. The test measures your blood sugar (glucose) and your risk of developing diabetes. This should be part of your routine tests from age 45 onward.

Another check performed by the doctor is a skin check. They will look for changes in moles, freckles, or other marks on your skin. You should examine your own skin at least once a month to check for changes in color and circumference of moles. Nearly all skin cancers can be treated successfully if found early.

Remember to also visit your dentist and mouth hygienist once a year for a check-up and proper cleaning. Tooth decay and gum disease can lead to serious health issues if left untreated.

Today's Exercise:

Make an appointment to visit the doctor: Go to your doctor for a yearly check-up and blood test. Even if you are healthy, you can find concerning things like low vitamin D, low vitamin B, low iron, or your cholesterol starting to get a little too high. This is a 10- to 15-minute check-up that is priceless for peace of mind. Get your teeth cleaned and checked every 12 months.

Week 6: Food and Exercise

Daily Tips for a Healthier Lifestyle

As discussed in Week 5, our bodies are like finely tuned machines that need regular maintenance and check-ups. In the same way, we need to look at the type of "fuel" that we put into our bodies for maximum performance. Just as you cannot leave your car in a garage for months and then expect peak performance when you turn the key, your body also needs regular exercise to keep it in peak condition.

Day 1: Keep a Food Journal

Keeping a food diary will give you insight into what you eat and drink each day. It will help you to understand your eating (and drinking) habits. You may be surprised at the number of calories you consume every day unconsciously.

Keep the diary for at least five days. The diary should be kept with you at all times. You need to diligently write down everything you consume from the moment you wake up to the time you close your eyes at night.

Your diary should include the following information for every time you eat or drink:

- Food name: Be as detailed as you can, and remember to include all dressings and condiments. For example, coffee with full cream milk and one teaspoon of sugar.
- The amount of food or liquid: This may be measured in volume (one cup of tea), weight (two ounces of minced meat), or number (four eggs). If you are unsure, estimate.
- What time of day did you eat or drink?
- Where were you when you consumed the above? (Write down home, car, office or name of the restaurant).
- Who was with you? Write down friends' or family members' names. If you are alone, note "alone."
- Activity: What were you doing while you were consuming the item? Were you driving, watching TV, at your desk, or chatting to friends?
- Your mood: Include how you were feeling while consuming the item.

For a food journal to be successful you need to be brutally honest. You will only be cheating yourself by omitting or adding certain items. The idea is to give you insight into your eating habits, you may for example, discover that you eat chocolate at your desk at 3 p.m. every afternoon, which may be an indicator of low blood sugar at that specific time. It will help you understand what choices you can make that will be healthier.

Today's Exercise:

Track your intake: What do you usually have for lunch while you work. Is it healthy? Keep a food journal for 48 hours and analyze it. What is working well? What would you like to improve? What can you cut down on? Did you skip any meals?

Day 2: Healthier Options

Once you understand what you are eating each day by keeping a food journal, you can start to make healthier choices. When choosing foods from the five main food groups, keep the following in mind:

- Grains: Choose whole grains when possible as they are high in fiber and low in fat which means they are low GI (glycemic index) and will keep you feeling full for longer. Try to avoid foods such as pastries, rolls, and muffins as these often contain refined flour and are high in sugar. Remember, grains are metabolized to sugar.
- Fruits and vegetables which are naturally high in fiber and water and low in fat: They are full of flavor and contain necessary minerals and vitamins. Try to eat them raw or steamed in order not to lose the nutritional value.
- Protein: Most of the protein we consume is derived from animal products. Try to avoid eating red meat more than twice a week, but rather, eat chicken or fish, or use non-meat options such as dried beans or lentils. When you do eat meat, look carefully at cooking methods, and use a minimum of oil, fat, or butter. Rather, dry fry or bake. Always choose the "lean" option

in red meat. In chicken, chose the portions with the skin already removed.

- Dairy: We can consume a large amount of fat without noticing by eating and drinking full cream dairy. Rather, choose low fat or no fat when choosing milk, cheese, and yogurt. Dairy is high in vitamin D and calcium which are important for healthy teeth and bones (especially in growing children). You may also investigate non-dairy options such as almond or rice milk.
- Fats and oils: A healthy amount of fats and oils are necessary for maintaining healthy joints, skin, hair, and nervous system, but too much or the wrong type may be detrimental to your health. Saturated and trans fats may lead to heart disease, high cholesterol, and diabetes.

Eating healthy should be a way of living. When buying food, healthy choices should keep your health in mind.

Today's Exercise:

Healthy lunches: Make a list of healthy lunches you like to eat at work that you can make at home. This can be anything from lunchbox whole wheat pasta meals to vegetable soup.

Day 3: Plan Your Meals

By preparing your meals a week in advance, you will have more time to spend with your family or a hobby after work. The benefits of preparing meals in advance include saving time, saving money (as you don't shop unnecessarily), you can prepare healthy option meals instead of grabbing a pie or sandwich in the canteen, and it will reduce stress as it is one less thing to worry about.

It is a good idea to prepare the week's meals over the weekend. Different kinds of home-prepared meals are:

- Reheat meals—meals that only need to be reheated before eating
- Assemble meals—assemble the ingredients (don't cook in advance) and freeze for later.
- Ingredient-only preparation—chopping and portioning out of ingredients ahead of time.
- Batch preparation—cook a single ingredient in large batches and use it in different recipes (for example, cooking ground beef to use in three different recipes during the week).

Another benefit of preparing meals in advance is that you will need to plan your ingredients ahead and will need to go shop less often.

Today's Exercise:

Prepare your meals in advance: Arrange to go shopping or have ingredients delivered weekly. Prepare these meals on Sunday evening before the work week. This will save you time during the week.

Day 4: Exercise at Work

Many office-bound people sit at their desks for a large part of each day. This can lead to health problems which include obesity and even blood clots. There are a couple of things you can do to get moving while you are performing your duties:

- Exercises with your desk and chair: Use your desk chair to do triceps dips. Repeat 10 times (do not use a chair with wheels). Your desk can be used to do desk push-ups (repeat 10 times). Calf raises by holding on to your desk (repeat 10 times).
- Exercises next to your desk: Lunges, side lunges, single-leg deadlifts, wall sit, step-ups, jumping jacks, marching.
- Exercises while sitting at your desk: Oblique twists, seated bicycles, leg lifts, glute squeezes, seated leg extensions.

You may also consider replacing your office chair with an exercise ball or even using a standing desk.

Go for a brisk walk during your lunch break to really get your heart pumping.

Invite colleagues for walking meetings instead of sitting in a boardroom.

Today's Exercise:

Count your steps: Exercise at work. How many steps do you get daily? Download a step tracking application. Set a goal to get between 2,000 and 10,000 steps daily (while at work or traveling to and from work). Try some walking meetings. Make an effort to go for a walk at lunchtime.

Day 5: Group Activity

Group exercise is a very effective way to get fit, lose weight, and get a better body while socializing and having fun. There are many options of group activities to choose from, from formal spinning classes at the gym to informal walking groups in your neighborhood. The choice of what and where to join in is up to you.

Some of the benefits of group exercise are

- Accountability and support: If you know people are counting on you as part of a team, you will be more likely to push through even on the days you don't feel like exercising. It is also very valuable to share your challenges with your exercise partners as they are the best people to motivate you to keep going.
- Social opportunities: You will meet people with the same interest in a relaxed environment, and you may even make new friends or meet a potential partner.
- Your leader is a professional: If you join a formal training program (such as a Pilates class) your instructor needs to be qualified to teach the activity. They will be prepared and offer more variety to the

exercise regime than you would have been able to on your own.

- Endorphin rush: According to a 2016 study (Johnson, 2016) socializing increases endorphin (the feel-good hormone) output. Exercise does the same, so by combining the two you are bound to feel great after exercising in a group.
- Affordable: A group class is more affordable than an individual session.

Today's Exercise:

Join in: Join one group activity sports class each week. This can be an evening walking club, beginner tennis lessons, any local sport you perhaps played as a child but then stopped, or a new sport you would like to try.

Week 7: Reduce Stress Outside of Work

The first rule of management is delegation. Don't try and do everything yourself because you can't. – Anthea Turner

---

Daily Tips to Help You Delegate

Being a manager is often a full-time and stressful job. It will benefit your physical and mental health if you can reduce some of the stress you experience outside of work. By reducing your responsibilities away from work you will find you have more time to relax and do the things you love instead of being bogged down with more chores.

Learning to delegate is an important management skill that you as a manager use regularly to complete projects and tasks on time. Now you can use the same skill to simplify your home life by delegating some of the tasks to professional service providers.

As when you delegate certain tasks to your team you need to be able to trust them to complete the task successfully, the same applies to delegating tasks at home. You will need to do the necessary research to find the most suitable (and trustworthy) person for the job. Remember, you want to reduce your stress, not add to it by having to worry if the service provider you trusted with your personal belongings will be capable of delivering the service they promised.

Day 1: Outsourcing Options

There are many home chores which can be successfully outsourced:

- Cleaning your house: Paying a cleaner for a couple of hours of work in your house each week can save you time, help you feel more organized and reduce your stress levels.

- Garden maintenance: During the summer you can hire someone weekly to mow your lawn, weed your flowers and water your plants.
- House maintenance: For larger jobs like fixed broken items, painting rooms, power hosing your driveaway and the million and one other to do list items you've got written down, consider hiring someone for a few days to do everything needed. Not only will everything get done asap, but as they are professionals it's likely they will do a better job than you ever could!
- Deep clean: Whether it be after renovating your property or a yearly occurrence, a deep clean is inevitable. Instead of spending a lot of money on cleaning products and spending your precious downtime cleaning, why not get a professional to do it for you? Professionals will use specialized cleaning equipment such as steam cleaners and rotary floor cleaners. The service often includes the deep cleaning of mattresses and dry cleaning curtains.
- Decluttering services: A professional will not only tidy up all your messy cupboards (from the kitchen to the bedroom), but will use containers and baskets to organize things in such a way that you will be able to maintain them.
- Food preparation: Hate cooking? You could hire a chef to batch prepare meals for you each week that get put into the freezer, so you have nutritious meals ready to

go every day of the week - no matter what time you get home from work!

Today's Exercise:

Identify tasks: Make a list of tasks that can be outsourced. These may include food delivery, garden care, laundry and cleaning, home maintenance, and pet care. Pick one task to outsource.

Day 2: Identify a Supplier

Word of mouth remains the best source of recommendations. If the service provider is trusted by friends and family, you can rely on them to give you the same service. Another good source to find a specific service provider is Google Ratings or on social media groups in your area.

Today's Exercise:

Do the research: Research to whom you can delegate the task. Research local laundromats in your area. Get a recommendation for a local home maintenance company.

Day 3: Take Action

You have done your research and have chosen a reputable service provider. The next step is to give the chosen task over to them. Remember that you need to give detailed instructions if you require anything out of the ordinary. You cannot assume that the dog parlor will know that your precious pooch has sensitive skin unless you tell them so.

Today's Exercise:

Take action: Drop your clothes at the laundromat, book in a home maintenance guy, or arrange food and household items to be delivered weekly.

Day 4: Tidy Up

There is currently a myriad of reality shows on television featuring hoarders and how they get assisted in tidying up their homes. It is insightful to see what huge emotional reactions the decluttering process provokes. Your home most likely does not look anything like the homes featured in the shows, but you may also experience the joys that tidying up brings:

- It offers a sense of satisfaction: Any action that gives us a feeling of accomplishment is extremely rewarding.
- Cleaning becomes easier: Clutter makes cleaning difficult (or even impossible). If the floor is littered with newspapers or laundry, the carpet underneath cannot be cleaned.
- Thinking becomes tidy too: Our brains are consistently taking in our environment. If your environment has too many stimuli taking up your thought processes, it is much harder to focus on tasks. In an organized, uncluttered environment your brain will be able to relax and focus on the tasks at hand.
- Improves efficiency: If you have to rummage through a cluttered wardrobe every morning to find something to wear to the office, you will be frustrated even before the

day has started. By organizing your home, you will not only save time usually used to search for missing things, but you will feel more relaxed and happy.

Once your "house is in order," you may find the momentum of organizing and changing carrying over to other areas of your life. You may be motivated to start with that job search you have been putting off or your organized kitchen may motivate you to cook those healthy meals.

Today's Exercise:

Tidy your wardrobe: Go through your clothes and throw out things you have not worn in 90 days. Then separate your clothes into winter and summer clothes. Make a list of what needs to be replaced and order the basics online if you can.

Day 5: Sorting More

Your wardrobe needs decluttering on a regular basis. You may fool yourself into thinking you have too many clothes (even though you are wearing the same three or four outfits), as many of your clothes may no longer be your size, are outdated, or just not be your style anymore. When organizing your wardrobe try to keep functional, timeless, and comfortable clothing with as many mix-and-match items as possible. Before starting to throw out clothes, ask yourself

- Why am I keeping this? It may be that you have not worn an item for many years, but you are keeping it because of the occasion it represents. It may be time to take the item out of your cupboard and put it in storage if you feel you cannot get rid of it.
- Will I ever wear this again? You may have bought clothes for a special occasion, and will not wear them again. Why not donate them to a charity where someone else may get joy from wearing it?
- Do I still fit in this? Many people have "fat" and "thin" wardrobes. Mostly the fat clothes are the ones being worn and the thin clothes are "for when I lose the weight." Unless you are putting plans in place to really

live healthier and drop the pounds, it may be better to say goodbye to your thin wardrobe.

Today's Exercise:

Plan ahead: Put the clothes you normally wear to work in a separate area of your closet, so that they are easy to find each morning. Plan out your day and clothes the night before to simplify your morning routine.

Chapter 8: Boost Your Team's Morale

Daily Tips to Create Positive Employees

As a manager, the "company culture" is your responsibility. A hostile work environment quickly leads to dissatisfied and unproductive employees, whereas a positive work culture converts to happy, productive employees. In times of crisis, the staff morale can make or break a company—you need to be able to fall back on your employees' goodwill to carry you through the hard times. Positive employees do not leave their jobs, and a low staff turnover means saving on training and induction costs for new employees. Happy employees are less likely to call in sick, will arrive at work on time, and willingly put in overtime when needed—all to the benefit of the company.

Before looking at ways to boost morale, we need to understand what leads to a lack in employee morale and what to avoid:

- Lack of growth: All humans are striving to better themselves and their circumstances. When an employee feels stuck and unmotivated, they will soon move on.
- If employees are unsure of what exactly is required of them, where they feel left out of the loop, or where expectations and goals shift constantly, they will become disengaged and will not be motivated to perform.
- A team identifies strongly with its leader. If the leadership suddenly changes, confidence may be shaken. As a manager, you should lead by embracing the change.
- One of the main causes of low company morale is poor leadership. Where a leader is too domineering and uses bullying and threats to elicit performance, employee morale will plummet and if left unaddressed, employees will move on. The opposite is also true, as a timid, insecure leader will quickly lose the respect of their team and a strong team member will fill the leadership void, often with disastrous consequences.
- Challenges within the company itself: If a company is known not to care about its employees, it will not attract

top candidates to fill the vacancies and a vicious cycle is created.

Day 1: Workplace Flexibility

In 2020 and 2021, during the COVID-19 pandemic, many companies were forced to have their workforce work from home as there were lockdown restrictions in place. Companies expected their employees' performance to plummet. The opposite often happened and most companies experienced a rise in productivity and morale. This phenomenon led to many large companies taking the decision to be more flexible about working hours and forcing employees to work from the office.

Workplace flexibility offers employees a choice of when and where they want to work. It gives an employee a better work-life balance which leads to better productivity and is thus a win-win situation.

We can differentiate between formal workplace policies where flexible work policies form part of officially endorsed human resource policies and informal flexible work policies which are made by a supervisor or someone higher up in the company on a discretionary basis.

Some flexible working arrangements include

- **Work from home:** There should be a policy in place on how many days in a week employees may work from home or if it can be done full time.
- **Workplace independence:** Employees are free to choose the manner in which they want to complete their daily tasks, but they are still accountable to deliver the outcome as expected. This is the opposite of micromanagement where employees are told step-by-step what to do and when to do it.
- **Flexibility in the workplace**: Where employees are office-bound due to the nature of their work (for example, retail), a company can still show flexibility by allowing employees to personalize their workplace.

Some of the benefits of workplace flexibility include

- The opportunity for the employee to balance work and home life. Employees can meet their families' needs (for example, attending sports matches on a weekday).
- Employees can work at a time they are productive (for example, late at night).
- The workplace (home) is more relaxed and the employee experiences less pressure. The employee can take a break when they feel tired and continue at a time they feel productive again.

- There are cost savings for both the company and its employees. The employee saves money on transport as well as possible after-care for their children. The company can save by reducing their office space and operational budget as employees can share office space by not being in the office at the same time.
- The employee has more time to focus on work-related tasks as they are spending less time commuting.

Today's Exercise:

Flexible or not? Research what your company's policy on flexible working hours is. According to CNN, a flexible schedule is very important to today's workers. For example, the choice to work from home and to choose their hours as long as they still deliver on performance. Giving your employees the freedom to choose when and how they want to work not only boosts morale, but can lead to an increase in productivity. Can you be an advocate for flexible working hours for your employees?

Day 2: Take a Break

As a manager, you may be under pressure for performance from your team. It may even feel counterproductive to have them do other things than work while they are at the office, but this is not true. Employees who do not take small breaks often and eat at their desks instead of stepping out of the office are more likely to suffer from health problems (mental and physical).

You as the manager should set an example that they can follow. Do not eat at your desk, but take a well-deserved break and leave the office, socialize with colleagues, or even go for a brisk walk around the office park. Your team will soon follow the cue and you will see a rise in morale and productivity.

A lunch break should not be used to troubleshoot problems or catch up on urgent work. Your employees should ideally be able to step away from their desks, hydrate and eat lunch, and get their bodies moving by walking for a few minutes before returning to their desks. This will ensure that both their bodies and minds are reset and ready for the next part of the working day.

Taking short breaks ensures that employees stay focused and do not become mentally fatigued, which will lead to a more productive workday.

A lunch break away from desks also gives employees a chance to socialize and catch up with colleagues. They will have the opportunity to interact with colleagues not necessarily in their departments which often leads to stronger collaboration and teamwork in the company. If your company does not have a room where employees meet for lunch, you may want to think of setting a space apart for exactly this function. It can take the form of a break room or weather permitting, can be outside. In this way, employees will spend their breaks as a team and not go off individually. By providing these spaces (and using them yourself) you will encourage your employees to do the same.

Research has shown that employees who eat at their desks are more likely to overeat and/or eat unhealthy food (Ogden, 2012). Employees who eat at their desks are not focused on what they are consuming, as they are most likely still focused on work (or even working while they are eating). They also are sedentary which means a missed opportunity to walk off the calories consumed during lunch. As well, inactive employees have a greater risk of becoming obese with the accompanying health risks.

Today's Exercise:

Short breaks: Around 62% of American workers eat lunch at their desks, according to a study by the Harvard Business Review (Wollan, 2016). We cannot function at our peak physical or mental capacity if we do not take a break at least for five minutes every hour. Ask your employees to take small breaks during the course of the day and after a week, ask them if they can feel a difference. This could involve grabbing a cup of coffee, taking a walk outside in the fresh air, or doing some stretches.

Day 3: Plants in the Office

Most people have an inborn desire to connect with nature. Even the most hardened New Yorker appreciates Central Park for the open space and opportunity to step out of reality of city life and into nature even if it is only for a few minutes. Unfortunately, most of us work in commercial office spaces and high-rise buildings that do not allow us to connect with nature as often as we want to.

A simple solution is to add plants to your working environment (be it office or home). Ask your company if they will be willing to sponsor plants for the office. Having greenery in your working space has several benefits, some are

- Plants make us feel more relaxed. The color green is relaxing and calming which makes green plants a sure choice.
- The Human Spaces Report (2015) found that two-thirds of employees did not have live plants in their office space, and those who did have plants, reported a 15% elevated well-being score and a 6% increase in productivity.

- Plants are pretty and make the working space more attractive for employees.
- During daylight hours, plants remove carbon dioxide from the air and replace it with healthier oxygen. A study by the University of Technology Sydney (Torpy, 2015) found that the impact of plants on oxygen levels is even greater in offices without air conditioning.
- Noise levels in offices are reduced when plants are present as they act as natural sound insulators.

When choosing plants, make sure they are meant to grow indoors and do not need direct sunlight (unless you are going to place them in a window).

Today's Exercise:

Get it growing: Buy some office plants (or get your company to sponsor some). That plants can make a difference in how we perceive our offices seems far-fetched, but it is not! Office workers with plants in their offices, or in windows where they can see trees are more relaxed than office workers locked in a windowless room without any connection to nature.

Plants assist with cleaning the air we breathe, and they are esthetically pleasing and an inexpensive way to brighten up any room or office. Unlike man-made air filters, plants work better over time as they grow bigger, and they are more cost-effective in the long run. Run down to your nursery and buy some plants that don't require lots of water or sun! (Moskowitz, 2008). Put them on your desk and invite your team to pop around and pick a plant for their desk if they would like one.

Day 4: No More Late-Night Work

The reasons for working overtime or after hours are numerous. All companies have times where overtime work is necessary and advantageous, but if working overtime or after hours is the norm to keep up to date, the red lights should be flickering. Working longer hours than expected is often linked to peer pressure. If all your colleagues arrive long before the official start of the working day and stay late to finish up work, you will feel obliged to do the same. If people working overtime or after hours are given positive feedback or recognition, it sends the wrong message to employees.

Overtime may also be used by employees to ease a financial burden. If a certain employee is constantly working and claiming overtime, you should enquire about the reason it is necessary and assist as far as possible.

Working overtime or after hours is detrimental to your physical health. The long hours of being inactive can lead to several health-related issues, from obesity to something as serious as deep vein thrombosis. The stress and perceived pressure that accompanies long work hours can lead to ulcers and other digestive issues, heart problems, and high blood pressure.

Long work hours also harm your mental well-being. Stress, insomnia, depression, overeating, and excess alcohol use are more common in people who work longer hours than normal.

An employee who is expected to work overtime or after hours will soon feel that their home life is taking a strain and this will lead to resentment toward the company. Job satisfaction will be low and the chances of the employee moving on increase.

How to avoid working overtime or after hours:

- Manage your time wisely, plan, and prioritize tasks. Complete your day's most important tasks early in the day if possible. Do not waste unnecessary time socializing, taking personal phone calls, or on social media platforms when you should be focused on your work. Tasks that can be completed at a later stage should be diarized for when they become current.
- Do not fall into the trap of helping out colleagues to the detriment of your own work. If you cannot assist, refuse to help in a friendly manner. You will be taking a lot of pressure off yourself and in the process, help your colleague to become more independent.
- Use technology to help you plan tasks and set reminders for due dates, as this will assist in scheduling your day and managing your time.

- Do not fall for peer pressure. If you are required to stay after hours sometimes, don't be stubborn, but stay and help out. Your colleagues should know that you are willing to step up in a crisis, but that you value your time and cannot be expected to constantly sacrifice your family, exercise, or hobby time.

Today's Exercise:

No more working late: Research if your team is working late into the night regularly. If they are, make a new rule—no work emails between 8 p.m. and 6 a.m. Trial it for a week and then get everyone's feedback on it.

Day 5: Celebrate a Holiday

Your company's policy will determine if and how religious holidays can be celebrated. These holidays should be approached with caution and while some people like to share their beliefs with others, many people prefer to celebrate in private. Where many employees share the same beliefs and the company chooses to let them celebrate (for example, a company with Muslim management and many Muslim employees may celebrate Ramadan). If the celebrations and special privileges (for example, leaving work early) are not extended to all employees, it may lead to some employees feeling excluded and even discriminated against.

It is safer to celebrate "the Holidays" instead of Christmas and focus on shared feelings, such as hope, peace, and the importance of family and friends. Some ideas to have inclusive holiday celebrations:

- Appoint people from different backgrounds and religions to form a party-planning committee.
- Use non-denominational holiday greetings such as "Happy Holidays."

- Keep decorations non-denominational (for example, red and green are accepted holiday colors by all religions).
- If employees feel comfortable with the idea, have a potluck lunch where dishes traditionally associated with the holidays are shared. Here employees can showcase how they (or the religion they represent) celebrate, which will lead to greater understanding and cohesiveness in the team.
- If you are celebrating together, remember to include alcohol-free beverages and vegetarian/vegan foods.
- Participation should be optional, as many people do not want to celebrate at work and their decision should be respected without question.

Today's Exercise:

Celebrate: Talk to your company about doing something fun for the next holiday event in your country. It could be giving every employee heart-shaped chocolate on Valentine's Day, or delegating someone on your run to organize a Secret Santa event before the holidays. Identify your next holiday, and delegate the job to someone who would like to organize it.

Week 9: Analyze Your Work Situation

Daily Tips to Face Challenges in the Workplace

We all expect our employees to perform to the best of their abilities and we appoint the most appropriate candidates to fill our high-performance team, but do we ever sit back and ask ourselves if we (or the company) need to make changes to achieve this? It will be unfair to expect a top performance from a team hampered by operational challenges. As a manager, you need to take a step back and analyze your team's operations and processes objectively and implement the necessary changes.

Some productivity killers are:

- Employees do not share your vision as they do not see the bigger picture. Every employee should understand their key performance indicators (KPIs) and how their part slots into the company's goals.
- Where productivity is lagging, it is wise to look at the supervisor. If the same theme or complaints are recurring, you need to investigate further. Find out if the supervisor needs more training or if there are any other challenges that they are experiencing. Include them in finding a solution and encourage open communication.
- Where communication is lacking, employees will not feel engaged and productivity will suffer. Remember, communication implies a dialogue, not one person talking and the others having to listen and comply. Your employees should feel that you are approachable and that they can vent their opinions without repercussions later. Make sure your employees understand the company's grievance procedure and have trust in the process.
- As a manager, one of the critical skills you will need is knowing how to delegate successfully. If you do not delegate enough, you will soon burn out. You should be able to trust your team to delegate even the most crucial tasks and that they will complete them successfully. If you do not trust your team enough to do

this, you should investigate the reason and make the necessary changes.

- If your team is not sure what is expected from them, or if you keep on moving the goalposts, they may become disheartened and in the end, just give up. Make sure you communicate all important information (for example, the commission structure) in person as well as in writing to minimize misunderstandings.
- A manager who acts inappropriately will quickly lose the respect of their team. Actions that violate the company culture and company integrity will cause disruption and a lack of performance. Inappropriate behavior includes sexual harassment, discrimination, stealing, breaking the dress code, arriving late for work, and getting involved in office politics.
- A team with operational challenges will not be able to perform at its best. Do your employees have the necessary equipment, is the equipment working, and do they know how to use it efficiently? The technology you are using may be outdated, so make sure that you keep up to date with recent developments and implement them where necessary.
- You need to acknowledge outstanding performance or dedication. If your team sees that someone has gone above and beyond and gets no recognition, they will not be motivated to do the same. The employee that

performs and is not recognized will feel undervalued and will be sending out their resume soon.

Day 1: What Needs to Change?

There are a few universal principles all teams need to be engaged in to perform at their best. If your team lacks one (or all) of them, you need to step in and effect the change. These principles are

- Core values. Your company's core values will be closely linked to its mission and vision statement. If the core values have not been listed formally before, you can make a list for yourself as a reminder. These values will decide who you appoint, how you will conduct your business, and with whom. Share these core values with your team and find out which of them resonates strongly and choose that core value as your mantra. For example, "families are important." This will remind them why they are passionate about what they do and will encourage performance.
- When to keep quiet. We get told all the time to voice our opinions and not to keep quiet, but maybe you need to let someone else take the floor. Listen to your employees' experience in conducting business. Let them tell you exactly what challenges they face without defending the status quo. You may be missing out on

valuable information if you are not willing to keep quiet and listen every once in a while.

- Be mindful of some elements of a process that may be frustrating or counterproductive to performance. Evaluate the process and see if it will be possible to eliminate or simplify the element that is causing friction. If the element is a crucial part of the process, explain it to your employees and ask them how you can make a change without compromising the process as a whole. They may come up with a solution, but even if they do not, they will understand why the element is necessary and will be more likely to comply.
- A good idea to measure employee engagement is an anonymous engagement survey. Ask questions like, "What is it about your job that you like the most?" "And the least?" "Do you feel valued by management?" and "If not, how can they change this?"

Today's Exercise:

Make the Change: Ask yourself if there is one thing that is holding your team back from achieving its goals. What is the one thing that you can change or improve that will lead to big results? This could be anything from a better process, faster Wi-Fi, the delegation of roles, or a change in responsibilities among your team.

Day 2: Resolve the Conflict

Conflict is part of any relationship, be it at home or at work. Some people see conflict as a breakdown in a relationship, but if the conflict is resolved in the correct manner, it may lead to greater understanding and a better relationship. Conflict is negative when it is ignored or when one party shuts down the other without listening to the opposite viewpoint, as this will lead to resentment. Conflict is associated with a range of negative emotions such as frustration, pain, discomfort, sadness, and anger. These emotions will form part of the relationship unless the conflict is resolved to the satisfaction of both parties. As a manager, it forms part of your job to resolve conflict within your team.

Follow the following steps to resolve conflict effectively:

- Identify the source of the conflict. Both parties need to agree on what the source of the conflict is. Ask questions to get to the bottom of the disagreement, and remember to focus on facts and not emotions. If emotions run high, give both parties time to cool down before attempting to resolve the conflict. It may be wise to let them work from home for the day. If this is not possible, try to separate them until they have calmed down.

- Find a private place to have a discussion. If you can take it out of the office, do so. Meet at a neutral space such as a coffee shop or a bench in a park.
- Set out the ground rules before the meeting starts. Acknowledge the disagreement and ask everyone to agree that they want to resolve the issue. One of the ground rules is "taking turns to talk'. Deciding on who is going to talk first, the other party is not allowed to interrupt verbally. Use terms like, "I hear you saying" and then repeat verbatim what the person said. Not only will you make sure there are no misunderstandings, but by repeating the words back to the speaker, they may reconsider the statement. Both parties need to "tell their stories" without interruption.
- Once both parties have voiced their concerns, you need to make sure you understand the issue. If you are still unsure, ask more questions, get the background on what led to the conflict, and acknowledge feelings. You need to identify the source of the conflict and both parties need to agree on the problem.
- Get both parties to commit to a common goal; for example, the project they are currently working on. Now they need to find a way forward, and how and what can they do differently to avoid repeating the same behavior

that led to the conflict. Here you need to sit back and let the parties come up with a solution and act as a facilitator when you see emotions flaring up.

- Remember that an issue that seems resolved today may raise its head again tomorrow. In this case, you need to remind both parties of their commitment to the project and the actions they promised to take (or avoid).

Today's Exercise:

Be a peacemaker: What conflict exists in your workplace that needs to be resolved? Brainstorm ways you can get this sorted out.

Day 3: The Big Challenge

We all have that one thing that bugs us in the workplace—the one thing that needs changing, but is placed on the back burner time and again. The issue may be with a relationship or an operational issue. Fixing the issue may lead to a jump in productivity. Often we get so used to dealing with the challenge, we are surprised what negative effect it initially had!

- Before fixing the issue, you need to identify exactly what the challenge is. Some issues are easy to identify (for example, a slow Wi-Fi connection), but some issues (especially if they involve relationships) are not as easy to pinpoint and need investigation.
- Once you understand what the problem is, try to determine the impact it is having on productivity. For example, a slow Wi-Fi connection may be frustrating in all circumstances, but if you are in the IT industry, it will be devastating. Find out what needs to change or to be fixed in order to resolve the problem (in the example above, we may need to upgrade our server or install a faster fiber line).
- Look at all possible solutions. Here you may ask for your team's input. For example, where employees

arrive late constantly without a valid excuse, involve the team to decide if there should be negative consequences for arriving late or if the early arrivals should be rewarded. If the solution needs a financial outlay (for example, upgrading the server), get quotes and follow your company's procedure for authorization. Do not delay—take action!

- Once you have identified the problem, understand the impact, and have a solution, it is time to implement it. The longer the issue remains a challenge, the more detrimental to productivity it will be as the team is now aware and focused on the challenge.
- When the challenge has been addressed successfully, compile an incident report outlining the problem, steps taken, and the outcome.

Today's Exercise:

Fix the issue: What is the one thing that is a challenge in the workplace or that makes you unhappy at work? Find three ways to address the issue.

Day 4: Work-Life Balance

Balancing your work and home life can create challenges. The first thing to realize is that there is no perfect balance. We will always be walking a tightrope, leaning more toward one and then more toward another. There may be times when you need to focus more on your career (for example, just before a project is due) and your home life may suffer. Similarly, you may need to focus on personal issues (for example, when your spouse is seriously ill) and you may not be focused on your career. The secret is to find an overall balance. If you look at the balance over the past six months (as an example) you should feel that you have attended to both in equal measure. Balance is measured over time and not day to day.

When your work and personal life are in balance, you will experience less stress, a greater sense of well-being, and a lower risk of burning out.

In recent years, many companies have realized that employees with a balanced work and personal life are less absent from work and are more loyal and productive. These companies have been investing in their employees' work-life balance as they reap the benefits. Below are some ways to create a better work-life balance for yourself and tips on how to support your team in theirs:

- Do not strive for a perfect balance, but rather strive for a realistic one. Remember, balance is measured over time. If you look back on the year, you should be able to tell if you were successful. If not, implement the necessary changes.
- You need to like your job. If you have to spend each working day hating what you do, you cannot be happy. You need to wake up excited about the day that lays ahead, not dread it. If you do not enjoy your job, it will flow over into your personal life too. If you are working in a toxic environment, or for a toxic person, or if you are not enjoying your job, it may be time to move on.
- Your health matters. If you are physically or mentally unwell, this will influence both your work and personal lives. Your body is not indestructible and if you do not take care of it, it will break down at some stage. So, have the check-ups, change your lifestyle, and do not be afraid to call in sick if you are not well. Overwork will

cause the problem to escalate to the detriment of yourself and your employer.

- Take time to unwind. You cannot let your work stress flow over into your family life. Find a way to unplug and unwind before opening your front door. This may mean reading a book on the train while returning home, stopping for a quick chat with a friend, or sitting in your car for five minutes while meditating.
- Go on vacation. Many employees do not take their leave days as they feel they cannot be absent from the office. You should encourage your employees to take a break, and they will come back relaxed and motivated to tackle a new project or task. With advance planning, productivity does not need to be impacted by the absence of even a critical individual.
- Prioritize your home life. You should be asking yourself what the main reason for working is, as many employees work in order to provide for their families—the same families that often are neglected in favor of work. Plan special family time, create a calendar for family and romantic dates, and stick to it. If you have promised to take your children to the zoo over the weekend, this should take priority over a last-minute project. Remember, any employee is replaceable, but you are the only mom or dad your children have and

they will be the people who carry on with your legacy, not your colleagues.

- Set boundaries with regard to work hours. Lead by example and set boundaries for yourself and your colleagues. When you close the office door, work should remain there until you open the door again. Try not to take work home to do after hours (if you need to in a crisis time, do so with caution). Consider having a computer for work and a separate one for personal use. Try to avoid opening up your work computer after hours and over weekends (leave it at the office if you can). If you work remotely, you may find that you are working longer hours than before as your home and work lives are entangled. Try to set specific working hours and stick to them. If you don't, you may find that you never stop working, and answering work-related calls and emails at night and even while on vacation.

Today's Exercise:

Analyze and change: What has your work-life balance been in the last 30 days? What can you change to improve this?

Day 5: Looking After Your Health (Again)

In Weeks 5 and 6, we looked at ways to improve your lifestyle. These included healthier meals, an exercise regime, getting enough sleep, and visiting your doctor for a check-up. If you have implemented the changes, you should be feeling better already. If you are still planning on implementing the suggested changes, read on for more reasons to do so:

- What is burnout? The definition of burnout according to Merriam-Webster (2022) is "exhaustion of physical or emotional strength or motivation usually as a result of prolonged stress or frustration." Burnout impacts your physical health in the following ways:
    - feeling constantly tired
    - frequent headaches and muscle pain
    - a change in appetite and sleep habits
    - lowered immunity
    - frequent illness
- Emotional burnout may have the following signs:
    - a sense of failure and self-doubt
    - a loss of motivation
    - a negative outlook on life
    - feeling trapped and helpless

    - feeling alone and isolated
- Some danger signs that are observed in people with burnout are
    - using food, drugs, or alcohol to cope
    - withdrawing from responsibilities and people
    - a "don’t care" attitude
- Prolonged burnout can lead to other mental problems such as depression and anxiety disorders. These may have dire consequences if not treated. Remember, prevention is better than cure.
- What are the risks of sitting too much? If you do not consciously move around during your working day, you may experience weight gain (especially around the middle, which is the most dangerous place to carry extra weight), and your legs and glutes will weaken which in turn will lead to back problems. Emerging studies show that some cancer risks are associated with inactivity. These include lung, uterine, and colon cancers. Research has found that inactive people have a 147% higher risk of suffering from a heart attack or stroke (Heath, 2015). Long periods of inactivity will cause blood to pool in your legs, and the build-up of pressure and fluid may cause varicose veins which may be painful and unsightly. One of the scariest consequences of sitting for long hours is deep vein thrombosis. This is a blood clot and is formed most commonly in the lower leg. The blood clot may dislodge

and travel to your lungs (pulmonary embolism) or brain (causing a stroke). These are major medical emergencies with long-term complications and may be deadly.

- The consequences of obesity: Anyone with a body max index of over 30 is classified as obese. (If you are unsure what your BMI is, there are many BMI calculators available on the internet.) If you are obese, you may be more likely to suffer from heart disease and stroke, high blood pressure, diabetes, some cancers, gout, gallbladder problems, breathing problems, and joint problems.

Today's Exercise:

Find the improvement: In weeks 5 and 6, we have looked at ways to improve your health. Have you followed through? Are you getting enough sleep, drinking water, eating healthy meals, and walking your steps every day? How has your health progress impacted your work? Identify one thing you can change starting today that will improve your health.

Week 10: Creating a Better Workplace

Most employees spend a third of their lives in the workplace. If this is a stressful experience, it will lead to mental health challenges and employees will leave to move on to less stressful circumstances.

As a manager, a big part of your job is to make sure that your employees are happy and productive. We will be looking at common challenges and try to find solutions to assist you in creating a better workplace.

Daily Tips to Create a Better Workplace

Day 1: Common Problems in the Workplace

Several problems are common in many workplaces. These challenges hinder productivity and compromise employee well-being. Below is a list of the most common problems encountered in the workplace:

- **Insufficient job descriptions:** An incomplete job description may cause misunderstandings, as the employer is expecting work from an employee who does not think it is their responsibility. Job descriptions should be reviewed as the operational needs of a company change and updated as necessary with the consent of both the employer and employee. Where additional work is added to the job description, the employer should compensate the employee accordingly.
- **Lack of training:** If an employee is not trained as part of their onboarding process, training should be provided at the soonest opportunity. Every new skill taught should be measured to make sure the employee is proficient in what is expected of them. Training should be provided by a professional and not an employee already proficient in the skill.
- **Ineffective job performance reviews:** Ineffective job performance is a situation where the manager has to tell the employee why they cannot expect a raise or a promotion. Its focus is on areas that need improvement

and often involves the manager talking and the employee listening.

- **Lack of employee recognition:** A manager needs to prepare thoroughly for a performance review, understand the employee's job description, and have a reasonable critique. Start the review with the employee's strengths and praise them for their accomplishments. Ask questions like, "What do you think your secret to success is?" and recognize hard work and effort put in. Then you move on to areas where the employee can improve. It is not good enough to tell a salesperson, "You are not making enough calls." unless you have monitored their calls and compared them with other members of the team to find the average. Where there are measurable outcomes, such as targets not reached, you should find out what the employee thinks the reason is and then discuss how this can be improved on. A successful performance review will leave both manager and employee motivated and in agreement on future steps to be taken, adjustments made, and clearly outlined performance objectives.

Where employees do not feel valued, they will tend to underperform and will ultimately move on to where they feel they are treasured. This is not only applicable to major achievements, but the little, everyday things as well. Get into the habit of saying, "Thank you." It takes only a minute to reply to an email with a *thank you*, but it sets the tone for a relationship that is conducted with respect.

- **No consequences:** As good performance and productivity should be encouraged and recognized, the opposite is true for poor performance. When a company allows employees to get away with poor performance (for example, regular late-comers), it dampens the motivation of the whole team. It is easy for one poor performer to pull everyone in the team's performance down to their level. Poor performance should be addressed, consequences set out (training provided if necessary), and if the employee is still not stepping up, disciplinary proceedings should be set in place to ultimately terminate the employment.
- **Excessive company policies:** A company should have the least number of policies possible. Policies should be set out clearly and be available to employees. Too many policies will smother creativity.
- **Facilities and equipment**: Facilities and equipment should be well cared for and in good condition. The capital outlay on facilities and equipment makes up a

high percentage of capital outlay. Set an example of how to care for the company's property; for example, equipment should be cleaned and neatly packed away at the end of each working day. Disrespecting company property will easily lead to disrespecting other company rules as well.

Today's Exercise:

Find solutions: Identify if any of the common problems are present in your workplace. If so, find three possible and workable solutions for the problem.

Day 2: Office Politics

Office politics are about employees using their authority or power to further their agenda. Every office has its office politics and you need not only be aware of it, but also how to navigate it. Even if you chose not to participate in office politics, you still need to communicate and work with colleagues and others in your company.

A few tips for not being intimidated by the undercurrents in the office:

- Build good relationships with colleagues and employees. You need a support network at work for times of crisis, and in turn, you need to provide support to those in need.
- Develop your social skills, learn how to read a situation, and anticipate behavior. For example, know which of the C-suite managers likes to be called by their title and who prefers to be called by name.
- Speak out when you see inappropriate behavior. Do not allow the office bully to flourish. Call out any behavior that does not correlate with the company culture; for example, if you hear some of your employees calling

someone names behind their back, reprimand them. Next time, they will think twice before doing so. Use your position as a manager to reinforce good behavior and lead by example.

There are a few things you can implement or focus on to change bad office politics:

- Build (and maintain) a positive company culture. Where employees feel valued and are proud of their company, it will be very difficult for bad politics to flourish. But where employees are dissatisfied or unhappy, it will take a small spark to light a big fire.
- Encourage open communication and resolve conflict as soon as it arises. Do not let bad feelings fester, as employees need to feel safe and valued. They need to be able to talk to you and not behind your back.
- Remind employees of the team's goal and reward small victories. If you are working on a long-term project, break it down into stages and celebrate the successful completion of each stage. Your team will stay focused and motivated.

If given the chance, there are certain office "politicians" who will step to the forefront and poison your team. They are

- **The Gossiper:** These people cannot keep a secret and love to share intimate details of others' lives with anyone interested. It may even be done under the guise of caring for the other person; for example, "I am so worried about Susan. She looks haggard. I think she is struggling after her husband left her for his twenty-something secretary." The best thing to do is not to encourage the gossiper. If you ask for more information, or act shocked at the information they share, they will carry on with greater force. In a friendly but firm way tell the gossiper that you do not discuss people where they are not present to defend themselves.

- **The Bully**: Small bullies (found in schools) grow up to be big bullies (found in boardrooms). A common denominator with all bullies is that the bullying takes place in secret or undercover. Corporate bullies may intimidate their victims by ignoring them, excluding them, threatening them, or spreading lies about them. Do not tolerate a bully in your team, but call them out as soon as the bullying becomes apparent.
- **The Climber:** This person is determined to climb the corporate ladder and will use you as a spar if they need to. They will exploit people and situations to their benefit without thinking of the consequences for the other person. They are usually "friends" with someone in management and like to drop names to seem more important.

- **The Advisor:** The advisor often already is in a trusted position and uses this to their benefit. When they are asked for an opinion, they will answer in such a way that the outcome will be influenced to their benefit.
- **The Credit Thief:** They take credit for other people's ideas and work while passing them off as their own. They will target younger and more timid members of the team and may even bully them into submission.
- **The Saboteur:** They are threatened by the success of others and will go to great lengths (and even sabotage) to make sure that they do not succeed. As with the bully, this behavior should be called out as soon as it is discovered. Do not let the saboteur take the power of your team.

Office politics may seem complicated and unsettling. Remember, you do not need to get involved and you can equip yourself with the skills to navigate it successfully.

Today's Exercise:

Do not fuel the flame: Do not participate in any gossip or speak negatively at work about anything for a week.

Day 3: Innovate

Often we are stuck with a problem because we believe we have tried everything and there is "just is no solution." The challenge may not lie with the problem, but with you being stuck in a certain way of thinking and not seeing any other way of doing it.

By looking at an existing problem with fresh eyes, you may find an innovative idea that will solve the problem. This may mean asking for someone's uninvolved objective opinion. Choose someone you trust (a good friend or family member). If they have a basic understanding of the business, it will be a bonus. Explain the challenge in detail to them, and allow them to ask questions (they may ask the obvious questions, but they may also ask a question that sets you on the road to a new solution). Once they understand the problem, ask them to come up with solutions. You may be pleasantly surprised, and even if you are not, you will be in a creative mindset to find an innovative solution.

To help you in the process there are a few steps to follow:

1. Identify the problem. Examine the situation unbiasedly (do not assume you already know the answer). You may need to reach out to an authority to assist you in analyzing the issue.
2. Find a solution. This may be a completely new product or process, or you may need to modify one that is already in existence.
3. Test your solution. See if it works. Build a cheap prototype of the new or modified product or test the new process on a limited scale.
4. Implement your process or launch your product. Measure the performance against the "old" version.

As a manager, you need to keep your team informed of what you are planning. If they need training in the new process or product, give it well before the launch. Explain to them why the new process or product will be beneficial to them and the company—get their backing before launching on a bigger scale.

Today's Exercise:

Find a new process: Identify one area in work that could be improved with a new process.

Implement the process and communicate it to the team. Remember to let them know what the issue was and how this process will save time, stress, and money.

Day 4: Paying It Forward

Together, we can change the world, one good deed at a time.
–Ron Hall

Paying it forward means doing something for someone out of gratitude for what you have, without expecting them to return the favor. You are paying it forward if you pay for the old lady in front of you at the grocery store, if you smile at the disgruntled businessman in the elevator, or if you take the time to pick up the stack of papers your colleague dropped. Every day presents us with many opportunities to pay it forward.

The good news is that giving is good for you, even if you don't expect any favor in return.

Giving (and doing charitable works) gives you a feeling of well-being and happiness as feel-good hormones such as endorphins are released. This leads to a drop in blood pressure and reduces stress—which makes it good for your physical health too. Furthermore, the giver's connection with society is strengthened by the act of selflessly giving as the giver feels part of the larger community.

Below are some ideas on how you can pay it forward at work:

- Appreciate your coworkers and tell them why. Do not wait for Secretary Day to say thank you, as a small gift will be much appreciated. There are members in every team working very hard behind the scenes to make it possible for you as a manager to excel—people like the cleaning lady, the janitor, and the security guard. Why not make an effort to greet them every day and on occasion thank them for their service? Just being acknowledged will make a difference in their day. Make an effort to find something positive about every one of your colleagues and tell them how you appreciated that trait. Bring coffee or muffins to the office unexpectedly to show your team you appreciate them.
- Step in if you see someone who needs help. If you know a colleague is struggling to meet a deadline and working overtime constantly, ask if you can help. Giving your time is often more welcome than a physical gift. Make a conscious effort to see where colleagues need help. It may be carrying heavy boxes or picking up documents that were dropped. Step out of your job description and become an empathetic human.
- Spoil your coworkers. This may take the form of you taking a colleague out to lunch, or paying for drinks for the team after work on a Friday. If you know a coworker is struggling financially, why not buy lunch for both of

you? If you are spending money as a gift, be sensitive that it is not seen by the receiving party as demeaning. Do it in such a manner that they feel they are doing you a favor by accepting.

Today's Exercise:

Pay it forward: The law of reciprocity means when we do something for a person with no conditions or expectations, they will be more likely to return the favor. Do something for someone at work with no conditions or the expectation of a return favor.

Day 5: Show Interest

It is important to get along with coworkers, as you spend a big part of your day in their company. If you do not have a good relationship with them, it will lead to unnecessary stress which is not good for your health. If relationships at the office are a challenge for you, make the effort to clear the air and resolve the conflict. You will not only be happier, but more productive and positive about your work. One of the best ways to build relationships with coworkers is to show interest in them as a person (not only in their work performance).

There are a few easy steps you can take to show that you are interested in your coworkers' well-being:

- Greet them in the morning and ask how they are. Make small talk for a few minutes before going into your office and closing the door.
- Remember facts about your coworkers' lives; for example, if a child was ill, inquire about their recovery. Share details of your own life, as this will lead to a discussion instead of you asking questions that may be intimidating.

- Acknowledge achievements, even if the colleague is not part of your team. A pat on the back will make them feel valued and appreciated.
- Do not partake in office gossip. If a colleague shares something personal with you and you break the trust by sharing with others, communication will not only break down with that colleague, but other colleagues will be scared to confide in you.
- When a new colleague joins your company or team, take time to get to know them. Ask about their circumstances and home life without being nosy. People quickly pick up if you are not interested in them.

Today's Exercise:

Be genuine: Be genuinely interested in other people. Find someone on your team and talk to them about something they are passionate about outside of work.

Week 11: How to Manage Remote Employees

Daily Tips to Face a Changing Landscape

During the COVID-19 pandemic that started at the beginning of 2020, many companies had to adjust overnight to employees not being able to work from the office. Worldwide lockdown restrictions were in place and movement was limited to essential workers.

This led to many employees being faced for the first time with working from home. Companies (and employees) quickly adapted and virtual meeting and training platforms boomed. When lockdown regulations eased, many employees requested to keep on working remotely and many companies agreed to the arrangement. Some companies have implemented hybrid work, where employees need to be in the office for a certain amount of time each week, but their schedules remain flexible and they can work remotely the majority of the time. Companies who embrace remote working quickly discovered that they are not limited geographically in appointing the best professionals they can find in their fields and thus, the remote team evolved into teammates working across time and space.

A remote team may imply that the team members are situated globally which means that they may be in different time zones and from different countries and cultures. It seems that almost all workers would prefer to work remotely or have the flexibility to work remotely at least some of the time. A survey from ConnectSolutions (2021) found that 30% of employees feel that they are more productive and complete tasks in less time. A total of 82% of the participants in the survey said that they feel less stressed and more in control of their lives.

Managing a team of remote working employees presents itself with its own unique challenges. As a manager, you are not able to call a meeting on the spur of the moment, as you will need to plan and invite your remote workers in advance to make sure they are all available. Their performance will not be measured in time spent working, but in output. You should set clear expectations for working hours, availability, communication systems, key projects and deadlines, scheduled meetings, and time to respond to emails.

Some of the challenges you as a manager may experience are:

- To measure accountability accurately and the difficulty in tracking employee performance regularly.
- The setting of clear boundaries, especially where some team members are from different time zones. Expectations with regard to delivery times may need to be adapted to take the time differences into account.
- Schedules need to be set far in advance and with everyone's time zone taken into account. Last-minute emergency meetings cannot happen with a diverse team working remotely. Thus, planning is more important than ever.
- One of the major challenges is to keep the team as a cohesive unit and to keep every team member feeling

that they are part of the team and not an isolated employee.

Some of the operational challenges you may experience in managing a remote team include

- The team will need to agree on which remote work tools to use. All team members will need to use and be proficient in the same virtual meeting platforms, such as Teams or Zoom. There are different online options for employees to quickly chat with each other, such as Slack or WhatsApp. It may also be worthwhile to look at project management software to keep your projects on track.
- You will need to find the most effective way for employees to be able to collaborate on a project. By just separating responsibilities and dividing tasks, you will lose out on the power of brainstorming and input from diverse angles. One option is to have weekly feedback meetings which take the form of every team member giving feedback on their part of the project and afterward, creating time for team members to discuss challenges and possible solutions.
- Plan and schedule key milestones. One of the biggest fears of any manager managing a remote team is how to ensure timely delivery of tasks to complete a project successfully. Here, accountability and transparency are

critical factors. A possible solution is to use shared folders in the Cloud where you as a manager still have access to progress in real time. Feedback should become part of the daily schedule before a team member logs off for the day.

- Just as in the office, it is important to schedule regular one-on-one meetings with remote team members. You may schedule "formal" meetings, but it is also a good idea to have a time each day where you are available to be called via an online meeting platform for a quick check-in meeting. This translates to a "virtual open door-policy."

Day 1: Feeling Isolated While Working Remotely

While there are many pros to working from home (such as flexibility, time saved on commuting, and independence), the one big drawback is that employees may easily feel isolated, disconnected, and/or excluded. As manager this will be one of your main challenges in managing a remote working team. Where communication between manager and team members is poor, team members will quickly feel disconnected and lonely which will lead to feeling unmotivated and productivity will suffer as a result.

Fortunately, there are several things you can implement to keep your team communicating and connected:

- Coffee connects: In an office environment, colleagues will often meet first thing in the morning at the coffee machine to get their early morning cup. This will not spontaneously happen with a team that works remotely and you as a manager will need to schedule informal get-togethers where team members can have conversations that do not involve work. Schedule your "coffee connect" and invite your team to join you. Remember, this is an informal chat. As this may be a strange experience for some team members, you may need to lead the first meeting by sharing a personal experience of the past week (for example, our dog had puppies on Monday night, and you can just imagine what is happening at my house). If you are comfortable to share, the other members will also share their stories.

- Question of the week: Another way for team members to get to know each other is to post one random question each week. Use the chat tool your team is using to post the question. Keep the questions short and sweet and not work-related; for example, "What is your favorite time of the year? Or give them a question they need to elaborate on like, "How do you spend your weekends?" It could also be a silly question like, "Would you prefer a unicorn or a dinosaur as a pet?" Remember to post your answer as well. You will get some interesting answers and learn a lot about your team members.
- Encourage group chats: If your team is very big, you may want to consider creating separate chat groups and to give members the option to join. For example, a group for "moms working from home" or an early morning virtual exercise group. These groups will help remote employees to stay connected.
-

Today's Exercise:

Lonely at home? There is a possibility that employees who work from home may experience feelings of isolation and loneliness during their workday. Creating informal opportunities for them to connect with one another is one way that you can assist them in becoming more productive.

Day 2: Track Your Workers' Progress

Teams working remotely come with many advantages (especially for the employees). One of the challenges involves tracking progress and productivity remotely. Below are a few ideas to assist you:

- Expectations and boundaries are important in any work environment, but where a team is working from the office, they are present for a set time each day, and performance is easily managed. The same is not true when a team is working remotely, as team members may live in different time zones and every member of the team is not necessarily working at the same time. Discuss work schedules with team members as well as expectations for feedback; for example, an email needs to be attended to within 24 hours, an employee may ignore messages until office hours, and virtual meetings will be scheduled at a time suitable to most. This may mean that certain remote workers need to attend meetings after hours.
- You may find that your remote team consists of a diverse mix of cultures (and even languages) which may easily cause misunderstandings that can lead to

conflict. Ask each employee how they want to receive feedback, and how often they want to check in virtually.

- Expectations and operational processes should be clear from the start. These include working hours, availability, communication systems, and scheduled meeting and response times.
- Your team needs to know that you are available to assist when needed. Remote workers may easily feel disconnected and may not have the assurance to ask for help. If you are in constant communication with your team, you will be able to pick up on the cues and address problems timeously.
- Invest in remote project management software to help plan the delegation of tasks, milestones, and deadlines for projects. The program should allow you to communicate with your team, track productivity, maintain timesheets, and allow team members from different time zones to interact seamlessly.

Today's Exercise:

Monitor remotely: Ask your employees for a work schedule along with tasks they need to complete by deadlines.

Day 3: Communication and Platforms

There are many communication tools for remote working teams available. You and your team need to do some research and decide which tool or tools will suit your unique needs best.

Below is a list of the 10 most used communication platforms for remote teams:

1. **Zoom:** Zoom originated as a conferencing platform, but is now mostly used as a meeting tool. There is a free version for basic use and a limited number of users and a paid version for professional use. It offers virtual meetings (with a time limit in the free version). Zoom's main features include video meetings (which can be recorded and stored), screen sharing, and an in-conference chat. Zoom is ideal for teams that require virtual conferences, meetings, and webinars.
2. **Microsoft Teams:** Microsoft Teams is an integrated communication tool with virtual meeting capacity, in-meeting chat, meeting scheduling, screen sharing, and recording of meetings (video and transcript). The tool

works well for small and larger companies that use Microsoft products.

3. **Google Hangouts:** Google Hangouts is a popular communication tool as it interacts seamlessly with other Google products (for example, Gmail, GDrive, and GApps). It also features virtual meetings and chats. The look and feel of the tool make it more suitable for informal meetings or casual conversations.
4. **Slack:** Slack is one of the most well-known and most used communication tools used cooperatively. Many remote teams use this tool as a "virtual Head Office" to share files and integrate tools. Slack works well for remote teams in different time zones and allows chats and channels for multiple users and departments. Slack does not have a virtual meeting option, but you can launch Zoom via the Slack platform.
5. **GoToMeeting:** GoToMeeting is specifically built for businesses as a meeting or training tool. Users cannot only share their screens, but collaborate by using the on-screen drawing tools. The tool also offers breakout rooms where employees can meet privately while a larger meeting is taking place. This works very well where certain team members quickly have to discuss an issue before presenting their solution to a bigger audience. The tool includes a feature called Smart Meeting Assistant which can answer questions and transcribe meetings in real time.

6. **Basecamp 3:** Basecamp (version 3) is a very popular project management tool. It works well for large teams with many tasks and projects running simultaneously. It features task management, a chat function, file and document sharing, and management as well as deadline and milestone tracking.
7. **Dialpad:** Dialpad offers talk (business VOIP calls), messages, and virtual meetings. It also offers a lead and contact center with a real-time messaging tool as well as automated messaging aimed at sales teams. It offers a dashboard to track lead follow-up and contactability which will assist managers in productivity and performance management.
8. **FreeConference:** FreeConference is a straightforward, no-nonsense virtual meeting and conferencing tool with a chat function.
9. **Gather:** Gather is a virtual communications tool aimed at making connecting more human and fun. Spaces can be customized and gamified (with avatars representing team members). It also offers private meeting spaces within a larger audience and even offers an option for remote working teams to create a virtual office from which they work. Virtual whiteboards can be used for brainstorming ideas and it is easy to share and manage documents.

10. **LifesizeGo:** LifesizeGo is the most basic of the tools mentioned and offers virtual meeting space for up to eight attendees.

All the tools mentioned above have basic (free) options, but if you are planning to use the tool for professional or business purposes, it is best to look at the higher-end options.

Today's Exercise:

Communicate in the manner they want: Ask your employees which manner of communication they prefer—email, texts, phone calls, video calls, or an internet-based communication channel. You need to find a balance between constantly pinging your employees with texts and emails and radio silence.

Day 4: Take Feedback to Heart

In an office environment, social interaction happens spontaneously—at the watercooler, over lunch, or passing in the corridors. If a team member is unwell, other team members will pick up on it. This intuitive empathy when someone looks under the weather does not happen as readily when teams work virtually. You as a manager will need to take the time to chat individually with each team member and you will need to ask the right questions and dig deeper if you suspect a problem. Below are some questions to encourage conversation and sharing:

- How are you feeling today? Rate your energy level. This is a great way to start the conversation as it can easily lead to a deeper conversation. It shows that you care about the colleague as a human and not only as a team member. Ask the team member to rate their energy level from 1 (non-existent) to 10 (high energy). This will give you an idea of how connected and present the team member is. If their energy level is low, try to find out what the reason is. If energy levels stay low for consecutive meetings, you should investigate further as productivity may be in jeopardy.

- What are the challenges you are facing? This is an important question as you need to address any challenges promptly. If the challenge is operational, it needs to be sorted out as a matter of urgency. If the challenge is not work-related, try to make plans or accommodate the team member as much as you can.
- What wins—big or small—did you have last week? Celebrate each small win with the team members. Each time they experience gratitude and praise, it will give momentum to the next achievement.
- What part of your role is most purposeful and which part do you find draining? By asking this question you will not only learn which part of their job they like to do, but you will also learn which part they do not like. This is the part you need to manage carefully as we all tend to excel in jobs we like, but procrastinate or avoid jobs we do not like to do.
- Is there a skill you would like to improve or develop? Most employees want to learn and grow to progress in their careers and it is part of your responsibility as a manager to help them do it. The company will also benefit from an employee who is upskilling. Thus, this is a win-win for both employee and employer.
- Are you clear on what is expected from you and how to achieve it? Employees who understand their roles and what performance is expected feel psychologically safe. If an employee feels sure of what they need to do, they

will get on with the job. If they are not sure of what is expected they may continue working, but at a slower pace as they will be unsure. It is your responsibility to make sure they have a crystal clear idea of what they should be doing and exactly what the expectations are.

- Do you like collaborating constantly or are there times you like to work on your own? It may be very hard for employees who crave company and collaboration to work remotely and they may feel lonely and isolated quickly. Make sure you create enough opportunities for team members to collaborate and socialize virtually. The opposite is also true, as introverts prefer to work on their own and only collaborate when really necessary. Allow them the freedom to work on their own, as they need space to develop their ideas.
- Is there a personal goal you are comfortable sharing? How can the company support you to make this happen? It may seem strange to ask a business manager to support an employee to achieve a personal dream, but when people feel valued and happy at home, they bring that energy to work.

Today's Exercise:

Check-In: Do a quick five-minute check-in with two of your remote employees to ask them how they are. Ask them if they need assistance or help or if they are experiencing any challenges. Take a minute to tell your employees that you appreciate their work.

Day 5: Celebrate Success

In a traditional office setting, celebrations are easy—buy snacks, drinks, and a gift, find a suitable venue, and invite your team. Virtual celebrations take a little more planning (especially if the team members are from different time zones).

There are many benefits of celebrating as a virtual team. Some of these include

- Team members feel appreciated and valued for their performance or on a special occasion.
- A virtual team does not have many opportunities to socialize, and a celebration creates such an opportunity.
- Team members get to know each other better which will lead to better connections and more collaboration.

A few ideas for virtual celebrations:

- **Celebrate achievements:** You may choose to have a weekly or monthly meeting to celebrate achievements. These can be milestones or deadlines reached in a project, a target achieved in sales, the team member with the most growth in an area, or the team member with the most sales. You may also include celebrations in scheduled meetings, and ask team members to share their small victories and celebrations.

- **Quiz night (or day):** Invite team members for an informal quiz night. You can use online sources for trivia questions. Divide the team into smaller teams (or for really small teams, participate individually). The winners can win a virtual gift voucher or if funds are limited, an afternoon off.
- **Game night:** Find a traditional board game's digital version and enjoy a night of games and fun with your team. You may even choose a theme (for example, Italian) and everyone must have snacks to enjoy from the specific country represented by the theme.
- **Virtual movie night:** Ask team members to vote for a movie they want to watch. Use your virtual meeting room to share the movie and chat or comment while watching. You may want to schedule breaks (to use the bathroom and to refill snacks) during which time socializing should be encouraged by asking leading, light-hearted, and even funny questions. Introverted members of your team will feel comfortable to join in and participate.
- **Virtual escape rooms:** For this challenge, team members will need to solve puzzles as a team to escape the room. They will need to collaborate as the

game is set up to encourage participation. One person cannot complete the puzzle on their own. Celebrate the successful effort as a team.

Today's Exercise:

Do it virtually: Start a new tradition by deciding how you are going to celebrate milestones online. The celebrations may be for the successful completion of projects or remote colleagues' birthdays. They may take the form of a team meeting where everyone is invited to bring a glass of champagne or a non-alcoholic beverage to the meeting to toast the success or wish their colleague a happy birthday. You may wish to design a special virtual background to be used for these "virtual celebration meetings."

Week 12: More Ideas

We have looked at what it takes to be an efficient manager, how to motivate yourself and your team, how to plan, different meeting styles, and a whole lot more. During this last week of the challenge, we will be looking at random things that can make or break you as a manager. Some of them may seem negative, while others remind us of business principles. Unfortunately, as a manager, you need to stomach the bad with the good. Not all of the below may be of interest to you, but it may be wise to take note of the information shared.

Day 1: Are Employees Resigning?

One of the hardest things to deal with as a manager is employees who resign. Even if you know that they are looking to move on, it comes as a shock and often leaves you as a manager with operational challenges apart from the emotional blow you may feel.

If an employee resigns out of the blue, it may shake your confidence as a manager. Looking back, you may have missed cues that the employee was unhappy or looking to move on. If you had seen the signs, you may have had a chance to address their concerns in time.

Nearly all employees who quit without warning show signs of disengaging with the team and company long before their resignation letter is written. If you as a manager can identify when employees are becoming disengaged, you may avoid losing them.

Signs of disengagement:

- **Productivity slump:** When an employee who usually delivers work of a high quality starts to produce work full of errors and submit it late, you should investigate. It may be that the employee is experiencing a crisis in their personal life and the slump is temporary. But it may also be a sign of burnout and stress.
- **Keeping quiet:** An employee who usually engages during meetings falling silent suddenly should raise a red flag that needs probing.
- **Resistance:** A normally compliant employee who all of a sudden acts aggressively or refuses assignments

may be ready to quit. Many employees "just don't care" before they hand in their notice.

- **Frequent absences from work:** If an employee is frequently missing while they are supposed to be working and gives no explanation, they may be attending interviews for another position. Or it may be that they are so demoralized that they just don't care to even show up.

If you have a feeling that an employee may be disengaging and could be thinking of resigning, you may want to consider

- Was there a promotion that the person wanted for which they were overlooked?
- Did the employee not receive a raise or bonus as they expected to?
- Are other team members resigning?
- Has the management or leadership recently changed and implemented changes in processes?
- How long have they been with the company?
- Are they going through a personal or health crisis?

If you can identify the reason or reasons for your employee's change in behavior, you may be able to remedy the situation or at least motivate the employee to give it another shot.

Remember, it is easier to find a solution or compromise than to find and train a new employee. The most common reasons for an employee resigning are

- a bigger salary
- bored with their current position and/or no opportunity for promotion
- poor management

If you are engaging with your employees, you will know their dreams and ambitions and you will be tuned in to pick up cues of disengagement. Your employees will also feel that they can discuss their concerns with you.

Today's Exercise:

Identify employees at risk of quitting: Make a list of your employees or team members. Have one-on-one meetings with each of them and try to determine how satisfied they with their current situation.

Day 2: Principles of Management

In an ever-changing world where technology rules, it is valuable to revise the classical principles of management as set out by Henri Fayol. Henry Fayol was a French engineer who lived from 1841 to 1925. He developed 14 management principles that were published in his 1916 book *Administration Industrielle et Generale*. These classical principles are still taught today in business schools all over the world.

Fayol's 14 principles of management are:

1. **Division of work:** A manager needs to be able to delegate tasks to employees. If an employee is not proficient in the task, they need training and practice until they perform at a high level.
2. **Authority:** A manager should act with authority. With authority comes responsibility.
3. **Discipline:** All employees should follow the same rules and managers should set examples.
4. **Unity of command:** There should be a clear chain of command. If not, authority, order, and stability are threatened.

5. **Unity of direction:** Teams should have a clear objective or goal toward which they work.
6. **Collective interest above individual interest:** Team interests should take preference over individual interests.
7. **Remuneration:** Pay should be fair and in line with effort.
8. **Centralization:** Decisions should come from above, but open communication with employees should be considered in the decision-making process.
9. **Scalar chain:** Each company should have an organization chart indicating the company structure. Each employee should understand their place in the hierarchy and the chain of command.
10. **Order:** Each employee should be appointed in the "right place" for effective social order.
11. **Equity:** Managers should be fair and show compassion with justice.
12. **Stability of tenure of personnel:** Staff turnover should be minimized, as job security creates happy, productive workers.
13. **Initiative:** Creativity and innovative ideas should be nurtured.
14. **Esprit de Corps:** Team spirit, morale, and unity are the building blocks for a high-performing team.

Today's Exercise:

Evaluate yourself: Which of the 14 classical management principles do you implement and where can you improve?

Day 3: Common Mistakes Managers Make

Managers are people and people make mistakes. You are allowed to err as long as you learn from your mistakes and try not to make the same mistake twice. You may find things you do on the list below, but please remind yourself also of all the things you do right every day. If you have grace with yourself, it will filter down to your team and create a culture of compassion and understanding.

Some of the most common mistakes are

- Managers see team members as gears in a cog and lose sight of individuals and their ability to collaborate instead of following orders.
- Managers dictate and never ask for input.
- They do not take criticism well, especially if it is personal.
- They are harsh judges when things go wrong, but are slow to celebrate victories with the team.
- They kill enthusiasm and creativity with phrases like, "this is just not practical."
- They are threatened by strong team members.
- They make commitments they do not plan to keep.

- They live in fear of their own boss and transfer the fear to the team.
- They are focused on the short term and forget the bigger picture.
- They are ungrateful and never say, “thank you.”
- They blame their mistakes or shortcomings on others.

If you see yourself making some or many of these mistakes, take a moment and decide to do better. You can!

Today's Exercise:

Step up: Have an objective look at the mistakes you make as a manager. Write them down and make a conscious effort to do better.

Day 4: What Do Great Managers Have in Common?

We have seen some common mistakes that some managers make and may have admitted that we sometimes do the same. Now, let's have a look at what good managers have in common. Hopefully, you will see yourself in some of the habits effective managers share. If not, you will know what to strive for:

- Good managers help their employees to see how their work is important in the bigger picture of the company or organization. Employees have a purpose and a vision of why their work is important.
- Honest managers value their team's opinions, they do not feel they need to have all the answers, and are not scared to ask for assistance.
- Effective managers listen to the challenges and needs of their team members. They value each team member for who they are and not for what they can do. They celebrate victories with their team and get in the trenches to work alongside them when it is necessary.

- Respected managers make their teams feel secure. The team knows that the manager has their backs, even when they make a mistake.
- Dynamic managers understand what makes each individual in their team "tick" and use this to motivate them.

Today's Exercise:

Give yourself a pat: If you are doing any of the things that good managers have in common, you are on the right track. See where you can improve and try to add one good habit daily.

Day 5: Climbing the Corporate Ladder

Many young people who are starting a career believe that if they start at the bottom of a company, they will advance through the ranks and end up in the C-suite, successful and rich.

Unfortunately, it is not that easy, as climbing the corporate ladder takes time, hard work, dedication, sacrifice, and discipline, and even then the C-suite is not guaranteed.

There are a few things you can do to make sure that you are noticed and first in line to start the climb. These are

- You need to be willing to do what it takes. No job or task should be too menial for you. If a volunteer is necessary, put your hand up and help. Your attitude will get noticed.
- The best way to show your worth is through your work. Put your heart into every assignment, and do not be satisfied with second best.
- Network with purpose. Establishing a strong network in your industry will open doors and provide opportunities you would not have had otherwise.

- Avoid office politics. Do not gossip or contribute in any way to a toxic work environment. When dealing with difficult colleagues, take the high road and do not get provoked to drop to their level.
- Do not get discouraged if things do not work out as you planned. Chin up and try again tomorrow. Resilience is one of the secrets to making it to the top.
- Know the data. You will impress everyone if you keep on top of the numbers. You don't have to guess, but prove your claims with facts.
- Keep your end goal in mind. Make sure you have a clear picture of where you want to be and understand the milestones that must be reached to get there. It is not realistic to expect to be promoted from being the cashier to the CEO, but if you understand the steps in between, you can plan your climb.

Some of the hard truths of the corporate ladder are

- The most qualified person does not always climb the fastest. Your degree(s) do not guarantee a smooth climb. You will need to work just as hard as a team member who did not study. You will, however, have a better theoretical understanding of principles which, if used wisely, will shorten the climb.
- You will have to take risks. You may have to voice an unpopular opinion to make a change happen. You may

take a risk and fail, but without taking risks, you will stagnate.

- Be accountable at all times, even if it hurts. Take responsibility for your own decisions and shortcomings. Never blame someone else for your mistakes and you will earn respect by being accountable.
- The corporate ladder is not only climbed in the boardroom, but also on the golf course and in the pub. You will need to network and socialize to get ahead.

Climbing the corporate ladder is not everyone's choice. Some people have a vision and mission outside of work and work is just a way to get money for what they really want to do. Others may be entrepreneurial and not satisfied to work for a boss.

You may start your career convinced you are aiming for the corner office, but a few years in, change your mind and start your own business. Many very successful business people started exactly the same way. Find your own path, climb the mountain, and enjoy the rewards.

Today's Exercise:

Your vision: Where do you want to be in five years from now in your career? Do you have a clear vision and milestones? If not, sit down and plan your future.

Conclusion

In 60 days, we have unpacked teamwork, how to impress your manager, the secrets of successful meetings, how to motivate and inspire, how to look after your well-being, and operational challenges in the workplace.

Week by Week Summary:

In Week 1 we discovered relationships are important and that building and maintaining relationships can be hard work. We have discussed the importance of getting to know your employees and understanding their dreams and aspirations. We have seen how feedback provided to employees determines the effectiveness thereof. We reminded ourselves that as a manager you are responsible to develop each member of your team for their chosen career path. We looked at body language and the importance of a first impression. We have briefly examined how it can be a challenge during virtual meetings to read attendees' facial expressions and body language. We discovered that teams need to be built consciously to be successful. We explored how easy and dangerous it is to label employees.

In Week 2 we unpacked ways in which you can impress your manager. We have seen that you need to build a relationship and get to know your manager as a person. We discovered the importance of determining communication and feedback preferences when dealing with your boss. We looked at ways to make sure that you do not miss milestones or deadlines by using technology to schedule important dates. We learned how your willingness to go the extra mile will make your boss notice you. We learned the importance of being a problem solver and not part of the problem itself and the importance of not just complaining, but being solution-driven.

Week 3 was dedicated to making meetings short and fun. We discovered the different kinds of meetings (from quick check-ins to walking and standing meetings) and every meetings' features. We looked at the new trend of "walk and talk" meetings and how exercise can be combined with serious discussion. We found out that attendees do not need to sit down during meetings, but that it is sometimes more effective to have everyone standing during a short meeting. We explored the secret of public praise and how this can raise the morale of a team. We learned that meeting protocols are still in use on occasion and we took note of the format and requirements.

During Week 4 we discovered how to keep a team motivated by working alongside them. We discovered how charity or volunteer work can help a team to bond and feel that they are making a difference. We explored the importance for a manager to utilize the skills of their team and to ask for and value their input. We looked at the importance of celebrating important days and holidays with your team and how having fun with your team cannot only motivate them, but enhance productivity.

In Week 5 we rediscovered the importance of sleep, hydration, and health on our physical and mental health. We learned the importance of and how to create a bedtime routine. We looked at the importance of taking in enough fluids and the consequences of becoming dehydrated. We unpacked the calming effect that water has on humans and how we can harness it in our working lives to help us relax. We were reminded of the importance of visiting a doctor for regular check-ups and not only when we are sick.

Week 6 was dedicated to food, exercise, and ways to create a healthier lifestyle. We saw how a food journal can keep you accountable for everything you consume and we found out that eating healthier need not be difficult. We looked at meal planning and ways in which to prepare meals in advance to make sure you eat healthy even on the days you come home very tired. We discovered that there is a whole exercise regime that can fit into short time slots and that you do not need to leave the office to exercise. We found out that group exercise activities have many benefits and were encouraged to join in.

In Week 7 we explored the importance of being able to delegate. We saw that many household chores can be outsourced (from the hanging of art to the yearly deep clean). We looked at steps to take to identify and implement the outsourcing solutions. We found out that a tidy environment helps to create order in your mind and that a disorderly environment can create mental stress.

During Week 8 we discovered that positive and happy employees are productive, creative, and willing to face challenges head-on. We looked at how a flexible work environment can lead to a rise in productivity and morale.

We found out that it is necessary to take short breaks often during a work day and that lunch breaks should not be spent catching up on work. We explored the value of stepping outside to experience nature and how we can bring a little bit of nature back with us by having plants in the office. We learned how working long hours is detrimental to our health and not conducive to productivity. We unpacked the value of celebrating holidays at the office, the value of learning to appreciate a diverse community, and the importance of being inclusive in our celebrations.

In Week 9 we analyzed our work situation. We found out that there are universal principles to engaging your employees and that conflict that is resolved correctly can lead to greater understanding and a better relationship. We looked at the challenges that we may face in the workplace and identified steps that we can take to overcome them. We unpacked the importance of work-life balance and how there are no quick fixes, but many small ways that can help you do better. We discovered that burnout is not just a feeling, but that it impacts your physical and mental health in many ways.

The focus in Week 10 was on how to create a better workplace. We looked at common problems in the workplace, such as insufficient job descriptions, the lack of training, and the quality of facilities and equipment.

We discovered how harmful office politics can be and how its negative impact can demotivate a team.

We also looked at different kinds of office politics and learned how they can affect your team. We examined the possibility of looking with "fresh eyes on old problems" to find innovative and workable solutions. We explored the benefits of "paying it forward," not only to the receiver, but also to the person giving or doing the favor. We also focused on how showing an interest in your teammates can build lasting relationships and create a happy team.

In Week 11 we learned how to manage a remote working team and some of the challenges you as a manager may experience. We also discussed the possibility of employees feeling isolated while working remotely and we looked at suggestions on how to keep your team communicating and connected. We examined the difficulties of tracking your workers' progress while working remotely and shared a few ideas to assist. We discovered different communication tools and platforms suitable to use in remote working situations and we looked at the features of each of these.

We also focused on ways in which to build a relationship with team members even when they are working remotely.

We looked at which questions you need to ask to gauge their level of engagement and to determine what their internal motivators are. We also discovered that online celebrations are possible and shared a few ideas for virtual celebrations.

During week 12 we looked at the reasons employees resign and how we may pick up on cues to prevent them from doing so. We also delved into the past to rediscover Henry Fayol's 14 principles of management and how they are still valid today. We focused on common mistakes managers make and what great managers have in common. We explored the basics of climbing the corporate ladder and found out that the climb may not be for everyone.

A Few Thoughts From the Author

After learning all of the above it may seem that being a manager is a serious business filled with hard work and lots of responsibilities. While this may be true, it can also be very rewarding (not only financially) and a whole lot of fun.

There are many advantages of being a manager apart from the obvious step up on the corporate ladder. As a manager you will be involved in decision-making, you will have more autonomy and control over your work, and you will be often better paid with more career advancement and development opportunities than the rest of your team. Your career path and next steps should be clearer and if you have focused on building a network, you will now be able to leverage some of those connections.

Do not forget those who helped you achieve a management position. An arrogant manager who thinks that they have made it on their own will quickly be very unpopular. Stay humble and motivated and you will be the manager everyone wants to work for.

We have all heard about (or worked for) the "boss from Hell" (and hopefully will try not to be one). Some of the (unbelievable) real-life stories below will make you thankful to be working where you are, so maybe you can relate:

The "busy" boss: I had a boss who was always too busy to assist, or if she did, she made it clear that she was "stepping out" of some important discussion to do so. She was constantly busy with her phone and even told us that she had "multitasking" down to a fine art form. That was until the day I sat next to her in the boardroom, in a very important meeting discussing a proposal with a new client. As I looked down to make a note, I saw her typing away on her phone and to my horror, discovered that she was playing an online casino game. That was the reason for her constant "multitasking!"

The thieving boss: And then there was the time I worked at a lumber yard and there were constant losses due to thieving. Management investigated and all the employees were called in one by one, first to be interrogated and then to take a polygraph test. The culprit was not identified and the losses continued. Then, one night when the police were alerted of a strange light in the warehouse, they arrested the vice-president of the company who was caught with a truckload of stolen material. Best of all, the same vice-president had chaired the inquiries and ordered the polygraph tests.

As if bad bosses were not enough, I have had to deal with some very strange rules. At one company, you had to return empty pens and short pencils to the office manager before receiving new office supplies. At the same company, you had to ask permission for bathroom breaks and they were timed and noted.

And then we've all heard of the boring team-building events that no one wants to attend. But when you get a little creative, and tap into people's interests outside of work, you can end up having a lot of fun in the process. Below are a few times I experienced team building at its best:

Wear the T-shirt—Things will go wrong from time to time. But if you can fix and learn from them, they can be a way to build camaraderie in a team.

I managed the development of an online math learning program. As part of this, we had a math glossary developed. Each glossary term had a picture and an explanation. These terms were created by a separate team in a different country. One image was incorrect, but it was not spotted until our end client (who our company was working for) saw it.

It was meant to be a picture of a mathematical tree diagram. But instead, someone had used the picture of an actual tree! Of course, we apologized, fixed it straight away, and put in another round of checks to make sure our images were 100% accurate in the future. But a few weeks later when we were celebrating meeting our deadline, I arrived at work with 20 T-shirts with a picture of a "tree" on them. Our team thought it was hilarious and the entire team wore their tree diagram T-shirts all day. Never underestimate the power of a funny t-shirt!

A weekend in the country—A weekend away is a fun way to break down the barriers and let people get to know each other better.

I organized a weekend in the country, complete with a day's horse racing for a group of 25 people I worked with. This was not sponsored by the company, and everyone paid for themselves. The country house we stayed in was huge, old, and full of character. One lady nearly got stuck in the elevator and in another room the bath overflowed by accident, requiring some help from the hotel staff. We were all still up singing along and playing guitar until 3 a.m.

The next day, we all went horse racing, and that evening, there were some great stories of who had spotted the most winners on the day. That evening again, more music and guitar playing ensued. The entire weekend was a total success, everyone enjoyed it immensely, and everyone who missed out wished that they had been there.

We rocked it—Outside of work, it is likely people have lots of different and unusual hobbies. Some of the people I worked with had a music background, and so one year, it was decided that they would put together a "work" rock band. The idea was that we would rehearse one evening a week for two months, and then perform the best of the 70s and 80s at our Christmas party for one hour, before the DJ came on stage for his set. Work provided some funds to book our recording space each week (it needed to be somewhere soundproofed with an amplifier and drum kit that a normal band would use to practice in). Our band name was the "Anticipated Mistakes." The band consisted of four guitarists, one keyboard player, one bass player, one drummer, three backing vocals, and one soloist. So, it was quite a large band.

The band became minor celebrities at work, and it was a great conversation point.

On the night of our Christmas party performance (we were all dressed in 60s fancy dress), we had so many instruments plugged into the hotel's power supply, that within the first few seconds of starting playing, we blew a fuse and the room went silent and black. It was fixed in a few minutes by hotel staff, and we went on to play a legendary set that our entire company adored. The satisfaction, fun, and feeling of accomplishment and team building that band generated was incredible.

Being a manager can be a lot of fun, even if the fun is not planned or occurs as a result of a mistake on your part. Learn to find the humor in every situation and it will put a smile on your face.

I hope I have inspired you to become the manager you would like to work for. May your climb up the corporate ladder be smooth, as the corner office is just down the hall!

And one last note… before you go, I have a small request to make. I would really appreciate it if you could review this book and share your lessons learned. Doing so will help me a lot in getting this book out to other managers who can benefit from the tips and strategies I have shared. Thank you!

Enjoy the next book in this series:

References:

Bigham, B. (2020, March 19). *10 Questions to ask your hybrid employees to keep them engaged.* 15Five. https://www.15five.com/blog/10-questions-remote-team-focused-on-work/

Calin, A. (2017, October 27). *7 steps to building meaningful team relationships. Hubgets Blog.* https://www.hubgets.com/blog/building-meaningful-team-relationships/

Clayton, R., Thomas, C., & Smothers, J. (2015, August 5). How to do walking meetings right. *Harvard Business Review.* https://hbr.org/2015/08/how-to-do-walking-meetings-right?registration=success

ConnectSolutions. (2015, February 17). *ConnectSolutions survey shows working remotely benefits employers and employees.* Prnewswire.com. https://www.prnewswire.com/news-releases/connectsolutions-survey-shows-working-remotely-benefits-employers-and-employees-300036189.html

Creately. (2019, May 21). *Effective methods of innovation for your next great idea | Creately Blog.*

https://creately.com/blog/diagrams/methods-of-innovation-process/

Culver, A. (2021, August 9). *10 ways to totally impress your boss. Www.snagajob.com.* https://www.snagajob.com/blog/post/ten-ways-to-impress-your-boss

DEVELOPER, W. (2021, November 9). *Why lunch breaks are crucial to employee productivity. American dining creations.* https://adc-us.com/blog/why-lunch-breaks-are-crucial-to-employee-productivity/#:~:text=A%20lunch%20break%20allows%20employees

Dugdale MD, D. C. (2019). *Health risks of obesity: MedlinePlus Medical Encyclopedia. Medlineplus.gov.*

https://medlineplus.gov/ency/patientinstructions/000348.htm

familydoctor.org editorial staff. (2018, April 27). *Nutrition: Keeping a food diary - familydoctor.org. Familydoctor.org.* https://familydoctor.org/nutrition-keeping-a-food-diary/

Galea, D. (n.d.). *How to celebrate employee birthdays in the workplace. Blog.bonus.ly.* https://blog.bonus.ly/employee-birthday-ideas#:~:text=Enhance%20employee%20engagement

Gillihan, PHD, S. J. (2019, January 25). *The mental health benefits of tidying up. WebMD.* https://blogs.webmd.com/from-our-archives/20190125/the-mental-health-benefits-of-tidying-up#:~:text=It%20fosters%20clear%20thinking.

Gurchiek, K. (2020, April 30). *10 tips for successfully managing remote workers. SHRM.* https://www.shrm.org/hr-today/news/hr-news/pages/covid19-10-tips-for-successfully-managing-remote-workers-.aspx

Heathfield, S. M. (2004, February 28). *Tips for effective management success. The Balance Careers; The Balance.* https://www.thebalancecareers.com/tips-for-effective-management-success-1916728

Heid, M. (2020, September 4). *There's a scientific reason why water is so calming. Medium.* https://elemental.medium.com/theres-a-scientific-reason-why-water-is-so-calming-79ec1b3a3261

How to win friends and influence people: The best summary. (2012, July 8). Farnam Street. https://fs.blog/how-to-win-friends-and-influence-people/

http://www.facebook.com/vvvliet. (2018, May 16). *Henri Fayol biography and books, management principles guru | ToolsHero. ToolsHero.* https://www.toolshero.com/toolsheroes/henri-fayol/

Indeed Career Guide. (2021, August 18). *17 ideas for virtual team celebrations (with benefits).* https://www.indeed.com/career-advice/career-development/virtual-team-celebration-ideas

Indeed, E. T. (2019, December). *9 qualities of a good manager.* Indeed career guide. https://www.indeed.com/career-advice/career-development/good-manager-qualities

Indeed, E. T. (2021a, June 9). *8 ways to build workplace relationships.* Indeed career guide. https://www.indeed.com/career-advice/career-development/how-to-build-relationships

Indeed, E. T. (2021b, September 21). *How to manage issues in the workplace (with examples).* Indeed career guide. https://ca.indeed.com/career-advice/career-development/issues-in-the-workplace

Iwankovitsh, E. (2021, November 4). *The 9 best communication tools for remote teams in 2019.* Www.highfidelity.com. https://www.highfidelity.com/blog/best-communication-tools-for-remote-teams

Johnson, K. V.-A. ., & Dunbar, R. I. M. (2016). *Pain tolerance predicts human social network size.* Scientific reports, 6(1).

https://doi.org/10.1038/srep25267

Knit People Small Business Blog. (n.d.). *What makes a good manager: 8 must-have skills to be successful |* Www.knitpeople.com. https://www.knitpeople.com/blog/what-makes-a-good-manager-8-must-have-skills-to-be-successful

Kubala, J. (2020, May 27). *What percentage of the human body is water?* Www.medicalnewstoday.com. https://www.medicalnewstoday.com/articles/what-percentage-of-the-human-body-is-water#:~:text=Most%20of%20the%20human%20body

Kulakauskaite, I. (2021, March 29). *How to define the steps in your innovation process - Idea Drop.* Idea Drop | Idea Management Software. https://ideadrop.co/innovation-strategy/process-defining-steps-innovation-process/

Landry, L. (2020, January 14). *How to delegate effectively: 7 tips for managers* | HBS Online. Business Insights - Blog.

https://online.hbs.edu/blog/post/how-to-delegate-effectively

Laskowski MD, E. R. (n.d.). *Sitting risks: How harmful is too much sitting?* Mayo Clinic. https://www.mayoclinic.org/healthy-lifestyle/adult-health/expert-answers/sitting/faq-20058005#:~:text=Research%20has%20linked%20sitting%20for

Leone, Ph D, P. (n.d.). *Measuring the impact of a bad boss. Training Industry.* https://trainingindustry.com/magazine/jul-aug-2020/measuring-the-impact-of-a-bad-boss/

M, K. (2008, May 9). *6 reasons to drink water.* WebMD; WebMD. https://www.webmd.com/diet/features/6-reasons-to-drink-water

Madden, K. (2018a, July 12). *12 pointless and very real office rules.* Coburg Banks. https://www.coburgbanks.co.uk/blog/friday-funnies/12-pointless-office-rules/

Madden, K. (2018b, July 17). *11 outrageous stories about managers from hell.* Coburg Banks. https://www.coburgbanks.co.uk/blog/friday-funnies/manager-from-hell-stories/

Mason, M. (2021, May 19). *7 jobs around the home that are worth outsourcing. Homes to Love.* https://www.homestolove.com.au/7-jobs-around-the-home-that-are-worth-outsourcing-15860

Mayo Clinic. (2021, January 6). *How to add more fiber to your diet.* Mayo Clinic. https://www.mayoclinic.org/healthy-lifestyle/nutrition-and-healthy-eating/in-depth/fiber/art-20043983#:~:text=Dietary%20fiber%20increases%20the%20weight

Michail, J. (2020, August 24). *Council Post: Strong nonverbal skills matter now more than ever in this "new normal."* Forbes. https://www.forbes.com/sites/forbescoachescouncil/2020/08/24/strong-nonverbal-skills-matter-now-more-than-ever-in-this-new-normal/?sh=176240875c61

MindTools. (2009). *Building great work relationships making work enjoyable and productive.* Mindtools.com. https://www.mindtools.com/pages/article/good-relationships.htm

Moseley, C. (2009). *6 ways to improve communication between managers and employees.* Jostle.me. https://blog.jostle.me/blog/6-ways-to-improve-communication-between-managers-and-employees

Motsiff, D. (2021, February 18). *Top 3 signs of an employee quitting without notice.* Insperity. https://www.insperity.com/blog/signs-of-employee-quitting/

Our Lady of the Lake University. (2021, March 4). *6 types of management styles*. https://onlineprograms.ollusa.edu/resources/article/types-of-leadership-and-management-styles/

Pawar, S. (2016, November 10). *5 psychological benefits by daily stand up meetings!* Www.linkedin.com. https://www.linkedin.com/pulse/5-physiological-benefits-daily-stand-up-meetings-shekhar-pawar/

Pelta, R. (2020, April 2). *Stay connected while working from home & remotely: 8 tips.* FlexJobs Employer Blog. https://www.flexjobs.com/employer-blog/stay-connected-team-working-from-home-remotely/

published, C. M. (2008, May 21). *Green plants boost job satisfaction.* Livescience.com. https://www.livescience.com/2549-green-plants-boost-job-satisfaction.html

Roepe, L. R. (2020, May 12). *How to manage different workplace personalities.* SHRM. https://www.shrm.org/resourcesandtools/hr-topics/people-managers/pages/managing-different-personalities-.aspx

Russell, R., Guerry, A. D., Balvanera, P., Gould, R. K., Basurto, X., Chan, K. M. A., Klain, S., Levine, J., & Tam, J. (2013). *Humans and nature: How knowing and experiencing nature affect well-being.* Annual review of environment and resources, 38(1), 473–502. https://doi.org/10.1146/annurev-environ-012312-110838

Ryan, L. (2014, September 9). *23 things most managers do wrong.* Www.linkedin.com. https://www.linkedin.com/pulse/20140909142131-52594-23-things-most-managers-do-wrong/

Sandeep Kashyap. (2018, August 3). *A manager's guide to manage remote teams.* proofhub. https://www.proofhub.com/articles/managing-remote-teams

Sissons, C. (2020, May 27). *What percentage of the human body is water?* Www.medicalnewstoday.com. https://www.medicalnewstoday.com/articles/what-percentage-of-the-human-body-is-water

Smith, M., Segal, J., & Robinson, L. (2018, December 27). *Burnout prevention and treatment.* HelpGuide.org. https://www.helpguide.org/articles/stress/burnout-prevention-and-recovery.htm

Stahl, A. (2018, February 26). *Three ways to pay it forward at the office.* Forbes. https://www.forbes.com/sites/ashleystahl/2018/02/26/three-ways-to-pay-it-forward-at-the-office/?sh=6a21cf76ae9e

suni. (2000). *National Sleep Foundation.* Sleepfoundation.org. https://www.sleepfoundation.org/

Todd, S. (n.d.). *What is workplace flexibility? (advantages for employer and employees).* Open Sourced Workplace. https://opensourcedworkplace.com/news/what-is-workplace-flexibility-advantages-for-employer-and-employees

Tompkins, C. (2017, August 28). *10 most common problems in the workplace | Glass Magazine.* Www.glassmagazine.com. https://www.glassmagazine.com/article/10-most-common-problems-workplace

Trickle. (2022, January 28). *Why fun at work is important.* | Real-Time Employee Engagement & Wellbeing Platform. https://trickle.works/blog/why-fun-at-work-is-important/#:~:text=Positive%20interactions%20and%20enjoying%20time

Valamis. (2021, April 13). 1*0 types of management styles: which one is the best [2020].* Valamis. https://www.valamis.com/hub/management-styles

WebMD. (2002, April 12). *Health risks linked to obesity.* WebMD; https://www.webmd.com/diet/obesity/obesity-health-risks

Wollan, M. (2016, February 25). Failure to lunch. *The New York Times.* https://www.nytimes.com/2016/02/28/magazine/failure-to-lunch.html

Wooll, M. (2021, October 29). *How to navigate office politics no matter where you work.* Www.betterup.com. https://www.betterup.com/blog/office-politics#:~:text=positive%20workplace%20culture.

Made in United States
Orlando, FL
07 February 2024